W9-BMO-291

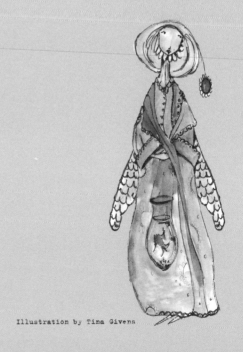

Illustration by Tina Givens

WHERE WOMEN CREATE
Quilters
THEIR QUILTS · THEIR STUDIOS · THEIR STORIES

JO PACKHAM

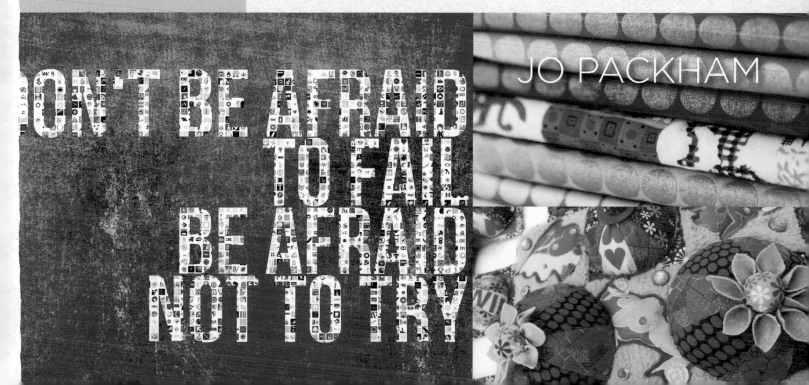

DON'T BE AFRAID
TO FAIL.
BE AFRAID
NOT TO TRY

WW PRESS

215 Historic 25th Street, Ogden, Utah

Production Manager: Brandy Shay

Copy Editor: Cynthia Levens

Designer: Matt Shay

Production Artist: Chelsi Johnston

© 2013 Jo Packham

First published in the United States of America in 2013 by
Quarry Books, a member of
Quayside Publishing Group
100 Cummings Center
Suite 406-L
Beverly, Massachusetts 01915-6101
Telephone: (978) 282-9590
Fax: (978) 283-2742
www.quarrybooks.com

10 9 8 7 6 5 4

ISBN: 978-1-59253-892-8

Each artist's 12" x 12" quilt square instructions are available for download at *www.quarrybooks.com/pages/women-create-quilts*.

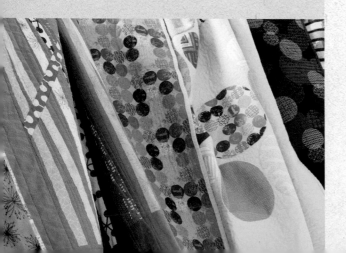

With each new title that I create, I meet artisan women and men that are so inspiring, so talented, and so giving of their talents that I am always just a little taken by surprise. How can so many artists create and share so much? How are there enough hours in the day to do all that they do with such forethought, planning, execution, and precision?

I would consider the making of just one quilt created by the designers on these pages or by the thousands of quilters around the world to be a lifetime achievement. Yet, these women and men create new techniques, new designs, and new finished quilts in numbers that I cannot even imagine.

And what is most remarkable to me is that none of us, regardless of how much we quilt, can ever fully understand the planning, the decision making, the execution, and the precision that goes into the quilts made by our fellow quilters — because each quilt and quilter is so different, each approach so individual, and each design so personal.

Unlike these artisans and the quilters in my family, I do not believe that I will ever create a finished quilt comparable to those on these pages or those that have been passed down through the generations in my family. But, I do want to thank each designer you will read about here as well as my mother, grandmother, and my aunt for their inspiration, heritage, and devotion to a craft. These designers truly are each a favorite and I am honored to represent them on these pages. I am forever grateful to each of you.

Much love always,

Jo

CONTENTS

Online Content

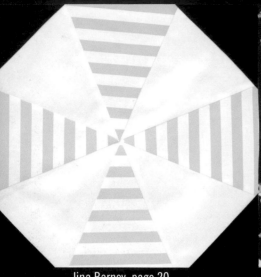

Jina Barney page 20

Amy Butler page 36

David Butler page 44

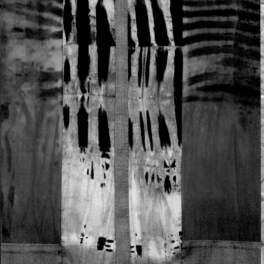

Judith Content page 52

Hoodie Cresent page 60

Tina Givens page 68

Heather Grant page 76

Alissa Haight Carlton page 86

Brigitte Heitland page 94

Learn how to create more than 80 quilt patterns with variations of the contributing artists' 12" x 12" quilt blocks. Online instructions can be easily accessed at www.quarrybooks.com/page/women-create-quilts.

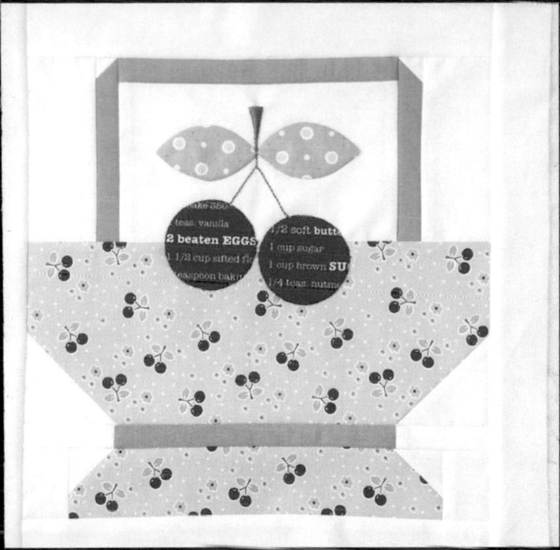

Lori Holt page 102

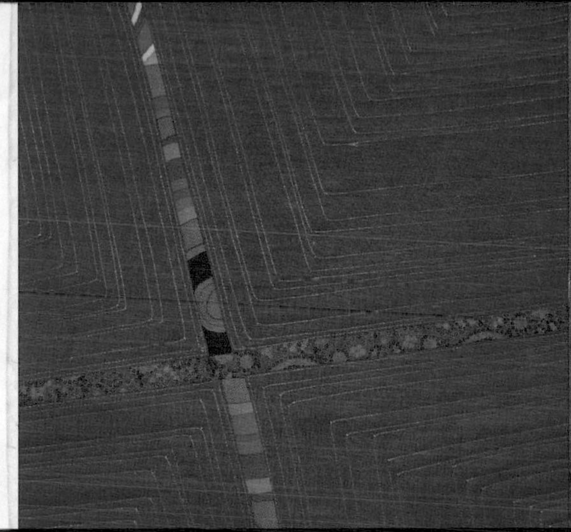

Leslie Jenison page 110

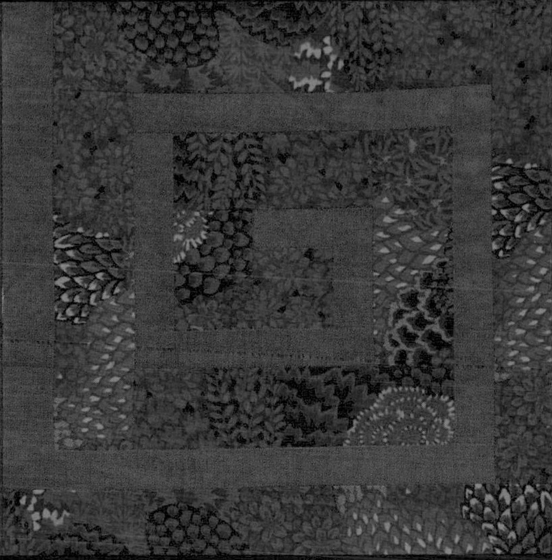

Liza Prior Lucy and Kaffe Fassett page 118

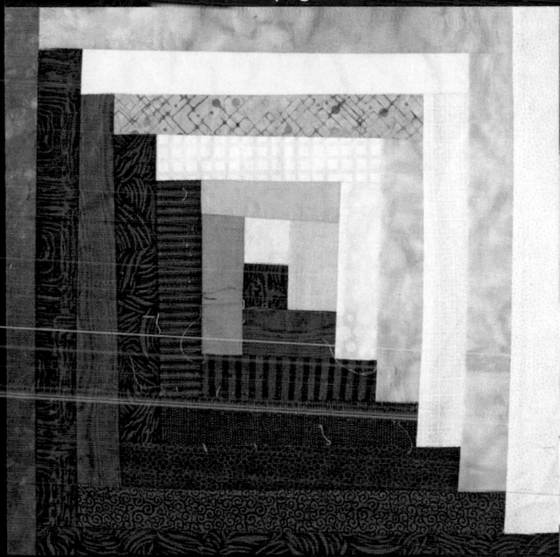

Katie Pasquini Masopust page 126

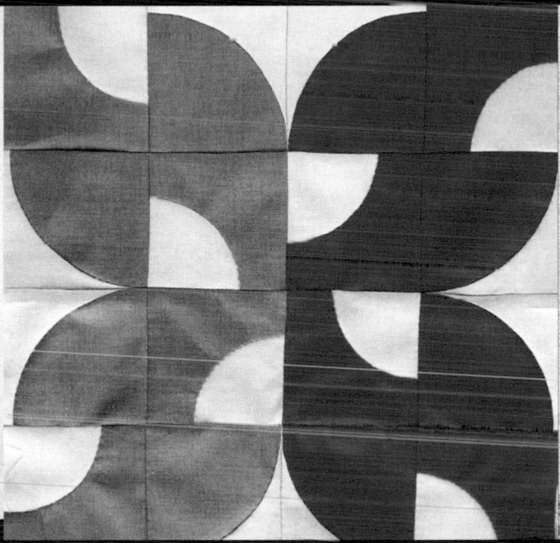

Kaari Meng page 134

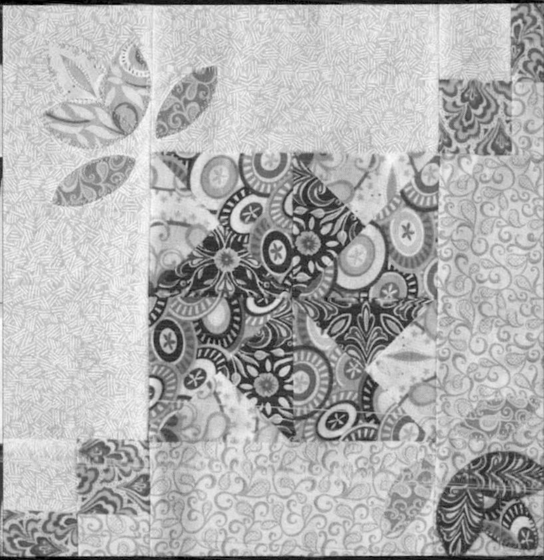

Amanda Murphy page 142

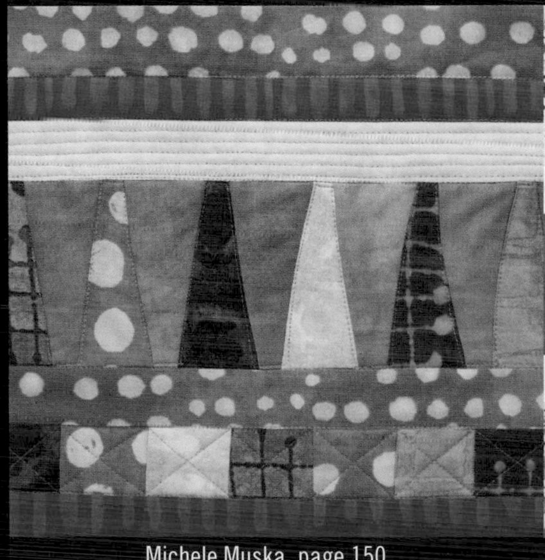

Michele Muska page 150

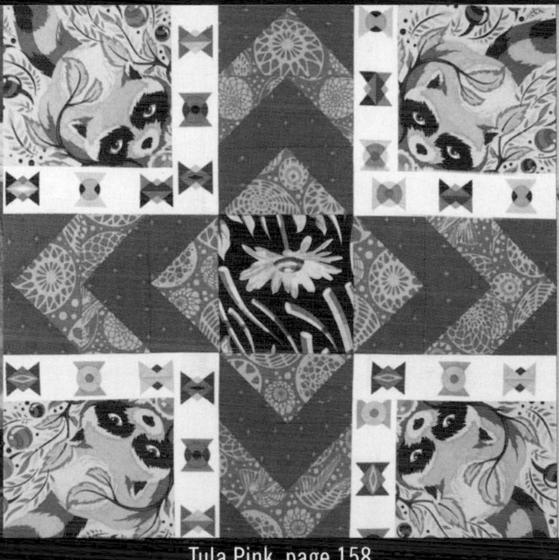

Tula Pink page 158

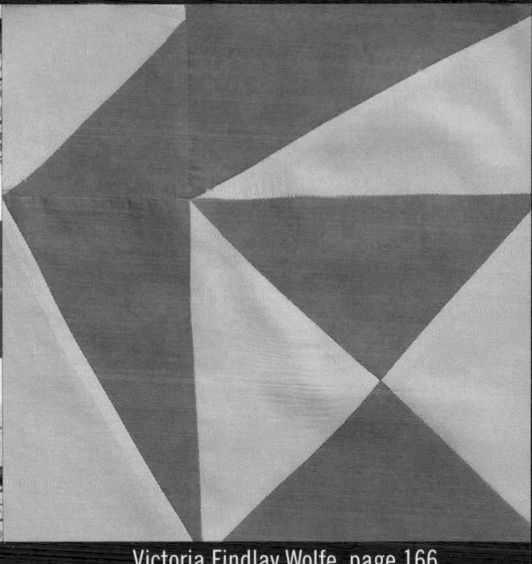

Victoria Findlay Wolfe page 166

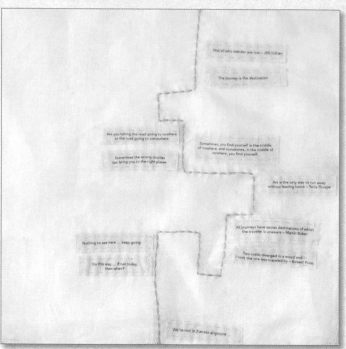

Jo Packham

12" x 12" QUILT BLOCK DESIGN

Jo Packham, creator and editor-in-chief of *Where Women Create*, has been a leading innovator in the handmade publishing market for more than 30 years. Her publishing company, WWC Press, is an imprint of Quarry Books. WWC Press also partners with Stampington & Company to produce the bestselling magazines *Where Women Cook—The Heart & Soul of Cooking*, *Where Women Create—Inspiring Work Spaces of Extraordinary Women*, and her newest publication, *Where Women Create BUSINESS—The Passion of Success*.

Jo has authored bestselling titles: *Where Women Create*, *Where Women Create: Book of Organization*, *Where Women Cook: CELEBRATE!*, and *Pieography: Where Pie Meets Biography*.

I cannot recall a time when fabric, sewing, and quilting were not part of my life. For as long as I can remember, I have loved textiles and all that can be created with them, especially the quilts. My childhood memories are seasoned with the color and texture of the quilts I slept beneath for warmth, worked on for pleasure, and appreciated for beauty. I have treasured memories of going through my mother's cedar chest and carefully unwrapping the tissue-protected quilt that my grandmother made for me before I was born — or maybe it was the quilt she made for my sister that was later taken from the cedar chest to shelter me from the cold winter wind. Either way, the quilts that were created by my mother's mother continue to be lovingly stored and gently wrapped in tissue in my own cedar chest.

My father's sister was the quilter in his family. I remember the countless hours she would spend cutting up well-worn, discarded shirts into pieces the size of postage stamps. It was magic to watch her create a quilt that would be used by anyone who was lucky enough to sleep on the porch in the spring when there was still a bitter chill before the sun began to rise. Even when I was so young, I would marvel at the precision and the patience that her work entailed.

My mother loved fabric too, but not as a quilter — she was an expert seamstress who, with no formal training, could create a prom dress from my grandmother's draperies, or a suit from only the memory of the day spent shopping together when I tried on the perfect skirt and blazer for baccalaureate. Much like the musician who can play a song by ear, having only heard the music once, she was enviable in her talent to create.

made by my grandmother

Yes, my practical, patient, and thrifty mother taught me how to sew. She showed me how to create a pattern for whatever I either wanted or believed that I needed, and she persistently taught me the lessons of "fine handwork." That meant, and still means, plaids perfectly matching at the seams, straight stitching lines, and a back as beautiful as the front, with no exceptions made for haste and no less-than-perfect craftsmanship.

I did learn my mother's lessons, but I have never loved sewing clothing like I love quilting. These pieced and quilted fabrics that tell the stories of the women who created them, the stitches that are so tiny you can barely see them, and the hours of creative, painstaking endurance that is devoted to making them, are what I love most. As stated in the forward of "The Quilts of Gee's Bend": "Quilting is a white woman's way of singing the blues." It's a quote I read years ago and have never forgotten.

I have always sewn my own clothes. In the early days, from necessity, if I wanted something then I had to make it. Now, mostly because of time restraints, I can just manage the altering, the hemming, and the embellishing of store-bought items that are not quite right. So I promise myself almost daily that when there is more time, my artisan soul will inspire me to make wearable art. Because then I can quilt, appliqué, bead, embellish, and sew, all on something that I can wear and not carefully wrap in tissue and place in my cedar chest for an unborn great grandchild to gently unwrap and wonder, "Why this quilt"?

11

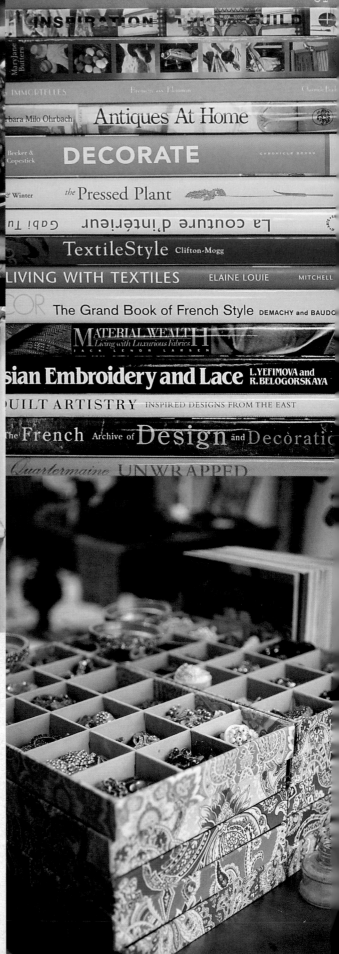

When I announced that Scott and I were going to marry, my mother knew that the only gift I would hope for was a handmade quilt. She gathered my grandmother's appliquéd squares that were still stacked in neat and even piles, and she had them quilted with a fabric of my choosing (which was a brown polyester/cotton blend that I loved at the time ... to this day, I am not exactly sure what I was thinking).

After Scott and I married and moved to Sacramento so that he could attend law school, I met a woman in an art class who once again brought a love of quilting to the forefront of my life. We spent hours and hours in fabric stores just looking at the possibilities. Martha was, and still is, the only woman I know that could spend four hours looking for the perfect collection of fabrics, go to lunch to think about them, and then return for another four hours to buy eight ½ pieces to begin her quilt.

During those three years in Sacramento, Martha assembled a group of creative women called Stitch n'Bitch. She and I were the only ones who actually did any kind of creative handwork, but we all would drink wine and wish the nights away. When I learned that I was pregnant with Sara, Martha insisted that each of the Stitch n'Bitch friends make me a quilt square so she could hand-quilt them together. Each friend loudly protested, but it was my only wish — a baby quilt with squares made by the hands of the women closest to me. Thirty-six years later, and I still have those squares.

Shortly after Sara was born, I took the quilt apart because it was so heavy and lumpy that it was impossible to use, and if the squares were framed I could hang them on the wall in the nursery. It didn't matter that true quilters would never recognize the handwork as quilting — these squares were wonderful then for what they were and wonderful now for the memories they keep. I made Sara lots of quilts before she was born, none of which were accurately cut, evenly stitched, or correctly assembled; but, I love them today as much as I did then. Now they too are gently wrapped in tissue in my cedar chest, holding the memories and daydreams of motherhood

Stitch n'Bitch

When we moved home and I began my publishing career, our first four books covered the most popular subject matter of the day — counted cross-stitch. However, unlike our competitors in the world of cross-stitch publishing, our designs were not only framed but also pieced and quilted. How could they not be? Every piece of handwork must be utilitarian — one cross-stitch picture per family is quite enough, but the need for one more quilt is both endless and timeless. And so, I added quilts, both new and vintage, to almost every book we produced. I found a way to include a quilt in our knitting book, hoping to introduce those who knit to the collectable world of those who quilt, and I created titles such as "Quiltagami," hoping to introduce and establish a new quilting technique so others who might have only worked in paper would love the art of fabric and thread as much as I did.

Throughout my entire career, I have surrounded myself with quilts, quilters, and quilting. I have purchased beautiful pieces and written books with, about, and for quilters. Doing this has allowed me the joy of not only the finished pieces but the process of hand- or machine-sewn quilting. Writing step-by-step instructions, photographing their work, and selling the publications made me a part of what they do and who they are, which is enough for me.

From its beginning in October of 1974, Karey Bresenhan's International Quilt Festival has been the place that I'd choose to be over anywhere else. I have only missed a hand-full of festivals over the years when life just simply blocked the way. Karey's brilliant assemblage of designers, quilters, and fabric manufacturers are such an inspiration to me, and to everyone there, on almost every level. I envy her, her dream, and what she has created for so many over the years and around the world.

I love the quilt exhibits at the festival — I stand in front of those quilts for hours just marveling at the planning, intricacy of design, stitching, execution, euphoria of accomplishment, and the dream of recognition. Each piece is, from my perspective, a lifetime work of art, yet these women create so many pieces that museums could be filled with just their private collections.

Not all who wander are lost – JRR Tolkien

The journey is the destination

Are you taking the road going to nowhere
or the road going to somewhere

Sometimes the wrong choices
can bring you to the right places.

Sometimes, you find yourself in the middle
of nowhere, and sometimes, in the middle of
nowhere, you find yourself.

Art is the only way to run away
without leaving home – Twila Thorpe

All journeys have secret destinations of which
the traveler is unaware – Martin Buber

Two roads diverged In a wood and I -
I took the one less traveled by – Robert Frost

Nothing to see here … keep going.

Go this way … if not today,
then when?

We're not in Kansas anymore …

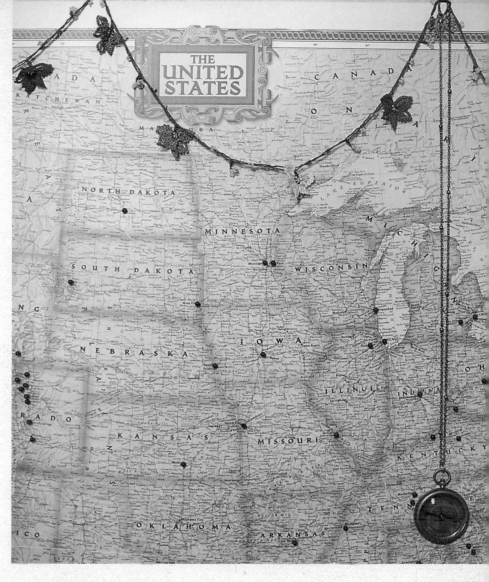

Favorite Quote

"The journey is the destination. Travel safe and
take lots of pictures!"

– Jo Packham

   I continue to write about quilts, envy the quilters, and buy those smaller yet intricate pieces that speak to me in hushed voices of their history and the stories that only they can tell. Will I ever be a famous, accomplished quilter? No. I simply do not have the patience or dedication required to become great, but I will sing their praises, photograph their work, and envy their accomplishments all the days of my life. And I humbly and gratefully thank each and every one of them for the stories told in the pieces of fabric that are so beautifully and lovingly pieced together.

To learn more about Jo Packham, visit wherewomencreate.com.

Jina Barney

Jina lives in Alpine, Utah, where her daytime occupation, as design director for Riley Blake Designs, is a three-minute commute from home. Her nighttime office is in the comfort of her own home. As owner and creator of Jina Barney Designz Pattern Company, Jina loves being around beautiful things and she is inspired by all that surrounds her. Her *perfect storm* is existing in the creative process, fashioning ordinary into beautiful.

I spent half of my childhood growing up in New Zealand and the other half growing up in Australia. I remember begging my mother to let me iron when I was a young girl. I would sit on the couch, with the ironing board positioned low so I could reach it, and iron napkins and doilies. I loved watching the iron take the creases out. It became an obsession. Little did I know that this was foreshadowing my quilting life ... an experienced quilter learns that ironing as you go can be the secret to having perfect measurements.

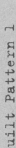
Quilt Pattern 1

Soon I was taking clothes off dolls and figuring out how to make my own doll clothes. My parents always encouraged my creative side by helping me to appreciate all forms of art. From a very young age, I was sewing and creating my own clothing. A dance scholarship took me to Brigham Young University, where I auditioned and became involved with the folk dance team. I was disappointed to learn that they deleted the fine arts program of fashion and design, so I graduated with a Bachelor of Science Degree in Travel and Tourism.

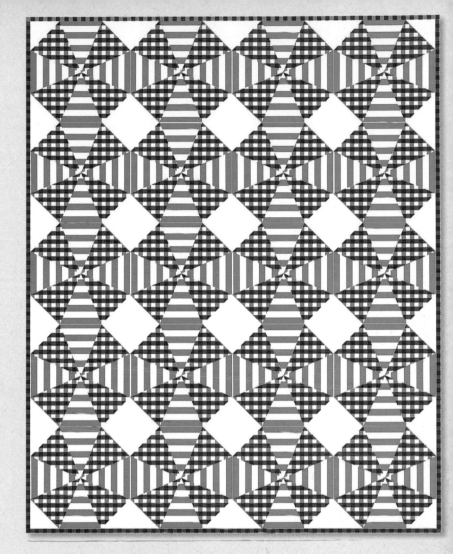

Quilt Pattern 2

As I began to have children of my own, I could not find clothing that I loved or could afford. I began drafting my own patterns and making my children's clothing. If they weren't wearing a big bow, they had a hat with big flowers and matching outfits. In my early 20s, I asked a friend of mine, who had just learned to quilt the previous year, if she would teach me and a few other people. We would put our children to bed and meet in the little red church in Alpine the last Tuesday of each month. We brought our sewing machines and taught each other to sew a block a month. There were eight of us in the beginning. Now, 25 years later, there are many more.

"I believe in pink. I believe that laughing is the best calorie burner. I believe in kissing, kissing a lot. I believe in being strong when everything seems to be going wrong. I believe that happy girls are the prettiest girls. I believe that tomorrow is another day and I believe in miracles."

– Audrey Hepburn

Quilt Pattern 3

Throughout the years I have made many handmade quilts for many special occasions. I was asked by a friend, who was dying, to make a quilt for each of her children. I organized this venture along with many friends' and neighbors' helping hands. We made five large quilts with embroidered sayings and words of love from a mother to her child. Each quilt was individual to each child. It was a labor of love and a miracle it was accomplished from start to finish in four days. I've always known that fabric is only fabric until you cut it into tiny pieces and piece it back together, but it's the story behind these quilts that makes them come alive and instill emotion and thought to everyone who sees the quilt and hears the story.

I launched Jina Barney Designz in 2007. I am also the owner and creator of Butterfly Kisses Pattern Company. These patterns are ideas and designs that I've incorporated from the clothing I made my girls when they were little. I started my pattern company with inspiration from my little niece Paige, who tragically passed away as a victim in a drunk driving accident. I thought it would be a nice dedication to Paige to name my pattern company in memory of her. At Paige's funeral we let live butterflies out of small packages and watched them fly away. Thus, Butterfly Kisses was born.

Quilting was a hobby and a passion, one that eventually led me to the opportunity to head Riley Blake Designs as the design director. I sometimes have to pinch myself — it seems like a dream. I now help create that same fabric I had caressed and loved into quilts for so many years before. My quilting journey continues as I create quilts for Riley Blake Designs, fulfill magazine requests, and design for my pattern company and, of course, my own children and grandchildren.

To learn more about Jina Barney, visit jinabarneydesignz.com *and* jinabarneydesignz.com/blog.

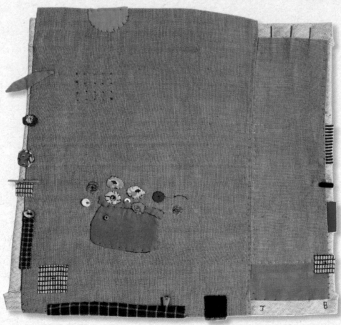

Janet Bolton

Janet Bolton grew up in a small village in the North of England. She spent the early '60s studying at an art school and then moved to London, where she still resides. After teaching art at a secondary school for years, Janet decided to leave teaching to be at home with her children. Out of necessity, she began quilting, found a style that was uniquely her own, and was caught in a whirlwind of success. Janet now exhibits and teaches worldwide and has published books for both adults and children. She believes that the life she lives came about purely by chance, and she is forever grateful for it.

During my time at art school in the 1960s, I took a printing course that introduced me to the idea of working with fabric in a free-form way. The emphasis was on machine-sewing, which wasn't really what I wanted. So although I loved the idea of working with fabric, I left art school and decided to return to my other creative endeavor, painting.

Soon after, my family and I moved into an old house in London. The house had draughty windows, so we needed heavy curtains to keep out the cold breezes. Knowing nothing about quilting, I tried my hand at making coverings. I began in the middle and worked my way toward the edges until achieving the right sizes. These pieces gradually became complete works of art. Through this practical need, I discovered my perfect working medium — developing ideas in fabric instead of paint.

Organic Cotton

In order to have spare money to buy fabrics, I set up stands at local craft fairs and sold small cloth purses and children's toys. To my amazement and delight, my framed pieces, which were the stand decorations, were very well-received! Nobody was presenting textile work in this way at that time. This led to being offered a stand at a prestigious craft fair. And that, in turn, immediately led to the offer of exhibitions. After I was approached by a card manufacturer and several different publishers, my exhibiting career took on its own momentum and has never stopped to this day. How very fortunate I have been!

These days, I have more time for teaching workshops, which I very much enjoy; this delightful activity takes me all over the world and has been the beginning of many lasting friendships. Although I would never describe myself as a quilter or an embroiderer, it's been a lovely world to be part of. Working from home has allowed me to extend all these activities and still enjoy being here for my family, my children, and now my grandchildren, which is very important to me. Nowadays, my whole house and garden have become my studio.

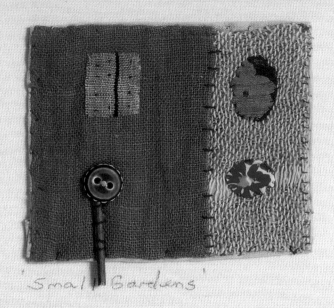
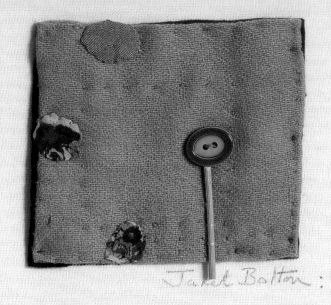

'Small Gardens'   Janet Bolton:

As to my working methods, I work in exactly the same way that I did as a child. A favorite childhood activity was making small, arranged gardens using flower heads, small stones, and sticks. The point being, that I build on my original idea from the actual materials to be used. The original idea is allowed to change throughout the process. My work is exciting to the very last stitch.

To learn more about Janet Bolton, visit janetbolton.com.

"I just put things together until they look right."
– Author Unkown

Amy Butler

12" x 12" QUILT BLOCK DESIGN

Amy Butler is an extremely talented, fun-loving, and creative spirit based in Granville, Ohio, where she works closely with her husband, David. Amy's philosophy of mind, body, and spirit is an integral part of her business. It is cultivated and carries over into everything she does.

Amy Butler's designs are soulful and most certainly vintage-inspired with a cool, cutting edge, colorful, and modern twist. She is nurturing her passion, following her dream, watching everything unfold, and experiencing endless joy from it all.

I feel like I've been pre-wired to love textiles — I grew up surrounded by quilt making, knitting, and fiber. My grandmother taught me how to hand-sew, and I spent many joyful hours in her attic studio. She had two sewing machines and would let me play on her ratty one, which was her daily driver. My appreciation for textiles grew from there.

I found myself in art school in the late '80s taking all the fundamentals, and by my sophomore year I was able to dabble in some more experimental classes. The minute I got into a fashion and textile class, a light bulb just went off. I grew a particular interest and love for global textiles. There's just something about a granny print floral and a colorful tribal design that somehow come together perfectly in my universe. It just all seems to go together so naturally.

Favorite Quote

"Let yourself be silently drawn by the strange pull of what you really love. It will not lead you astray."

– Jalaluddin Rumi

I really love vintage things too — that was the style of my mother's and grandmother's home décor and what I grew up with. When I was younger I thought that the old stuff was gross, but when I was in college on a limited budget, a thrift store was the first place I'd go to find cool and affordable things. Those vintage designs became a great source of inspiration, and I've incorporated them into my work ever since. They really strike a chord with me. Later on I began to collect antique documents, which found their way into my work as well.

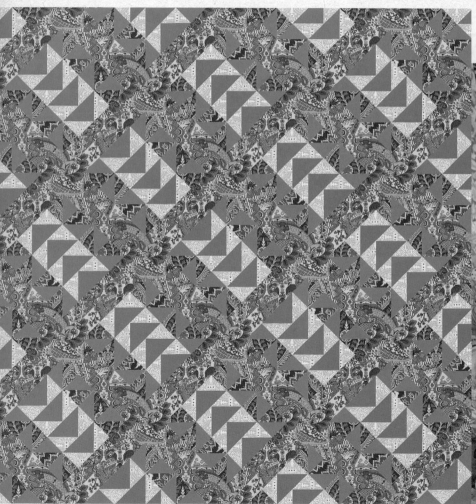

Quilt Pattern 1

Other than developing a passion for textiles, I also met my husband, David, in art school. We moved back to Ohio and rented a farmhouse that had a big space we could turn into a studio. We both started doing freelance work to make ends meet. Meanwhile, over the years I was always working on sewing projects and things to decorate our house with, mixing old and new fabrics together. Somewhere in there we connected with Country Living magazine and were producing stories for them as contributing editors. This is where my sewing and craft came together. One thing led to the next, I produced some sewing patterns, David laid them out, and they did well in the magazine. People began writing to us for more, and that's how I found my way into the quilt market.

I had my first little 10' x 10' booth and just thought to decorate it like my house. I had never done the trade show thing before, so it was all new to me and very exciting. A few fabric companies approached me, inviting me to design a fabric line, and one of them was Free Spirit. My first collection, Gypsy Caravan, came out the following spring. Eventually I developed the Amy Butler green logo brand, which is trademarked globally.

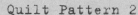

Quilt Pattern 2

It was about five years before we could afford to not take on any other freelance work to keep the cash flow coming. I always like to tell people that, because they think suddenly, overnight, you're rich and living your dream. It's a wonderful thing to keep in perspective, but you have to believe in what you're doing. Don't let fear and anxiety keep you from fully walking into your dreams.

I try to encourage people not to give up on their dreams, rather make them a priority and take time every week to paint, or draw, or whatever it is. As long as you are nurturing the thing that's in your heart, it's going to grow, but you've got to water it and give it attention. It's not just going to fall in your lap — you've got to make an effort.

41

Quilt Pattern 3

My latest endeavor is producing Blossom magazine in hopes of it encouraging others to step forward, bring out their gifts, create love, express beauty, and be kind. David's starting Parson Gray, and I really love the magic of watching him love what he is creating. We are constantly in a place of evolution; that's how it came together for us. I feel blessed because I get to nurture my passions and I actually get to make a living doing this. It just blows my mind!

To learn more about Amy Butler, visit amybutlerdesign.com.

Quilt Pattern 4

David Butler

12" x 12" QUILT BLOCK DESIGN

Ohio-based graphic designer, David Butler is a new breed of creative explorer. His many and varied interests include graphic arts, music, photography, fabric and product design, and even sewing. He is truly a Renaissance man in every sense of the word. Having worked for companies like Timberland, Ralph Lauren, Abercrombie & Fitch, and Hollister, David is ready to set sail. And his new brand, Parson Gray, is the flagship.

I have been doing graphic design for 25 years; I got into fabric design behind the curtain of Amy Butler, my wife. She needed somebody to help her with the computer aspect of design, and I learned fabric design to help her with production. I've spent the last eight years kind of behind the scenes of this industry. As a result of working closely with Westminster, they prompted me to think about doing my own line; there's a niche for male-friendly fabrics. I rolled it around for a while. I was just so busy with Amy's stuff that it took me a couple of years to finally pull it together.

Quilt Pattern 1

Parson Gray is the brand; it's the moniker that I use for my creative endeavors. In the fabric world, I have a folk-modern vernacular to my style. Amy really coaxed me along and helped guide me. My first line came out last year. Now it's kind of its own thing, which really feels great! Sales have been very good; people seem to get it. I think all you can do is create something that you would want to see in the market place — that's how it works for me.

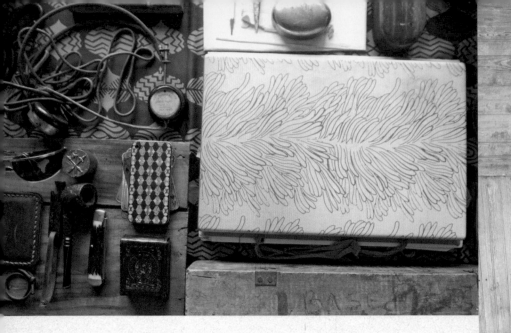

I've found that I like sewing, but I don't have a lot of time to actually sit down and sew. What I really enjoy doing is creating a box of crayons for other people to color with. That's the way I see my work in creating raw materials — I love to see what other people do with it!

Everything about Parson Gray is entirely my vision — it comes from my hand. I am creating the designs and doing the styling and the photography. I'm not a control freak, I just don't know any other way to do it. There's no aspect of it that I'd want to turn over to somebody else. I have a very distinct vision of the story I want to tell through the texture of the fabrics. It's all part of the romance and plays into creative storytelling. I want it to have a specific point of view.

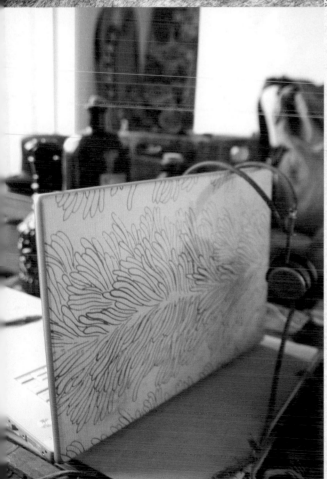

Quilt Pattern 2

A lot of things influence my work. I love world travel; visiting different cultures and exploring them is enriching. I've always been enamored with flags ever since I was a boy. My parents traveled and brought back little flags and banners for me. My flag designs hint of an old-world theme. You see the same type of design and pattern in quilts — the way the fabric is used to interpret a story like that of the Union Jack being a combination of England, Scotland, and Wales. It's pretty cool to pick apart the meaning behind flags' colors.

Because I've had a lot of requests for them, I've recently released my first downloadable flag pattern. I'm also working on a line of bags, which is a completely different realm from fabric, including masculine army duffles and military style bags made of waxed canvas and leather. The only pattern design is on the inside; it's actually one of my new prints shrunk way down as an interior liner. I'm also doing other things like phone skins. Going into the gift and fashion market is a whole different animal, and it's really kind of fun for me.

49

"Life in itself is an empty canvas; it becomes whatsoever you paint on it. You can paint misery, you can paint bliss. This freedom is your glory."

– Osho, Indian philosopher

I come from that world of creating shop concepts and product designs. I understand that world, but I haven't done a lot of the actual product itself. I like learning something new as I go and just rolling with it. That's the whole process of life I think. If you know everything, and if you stop learning, you're going to stop growing as a person. You have to be willing to jump into things that you might not be super comfortable with. You never know what you might encounter that you really love. And then that joy comes through, people get into it, and next thing you know it's a business. There's no silver bullet to having a successful business other than this: You're going to be successful if you're loving and enjoying what you do every day.

To learn more about David Butler, visit parsongray.com.

Quilt Pattern 4

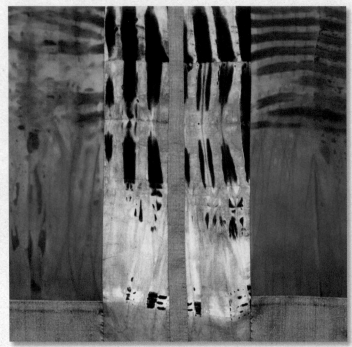

Judith Content

California textile artist, Judith Content, is never happier than when she's in her home studio. She begins her days with an early morning hike or gardening, after which she delves wholeheartedly into her creative endeavors and works until she is forced to quit late in the evening. Time passes in a blink of an eye as she explores her love of the classic Japanese Arashi-Shibori dye technique that has forever fascinated her.

My mind is always going with ideas. I am the product of an artist mother and an engineer father. My grandfather was an efficiency engineer, so I just love things to be eloquent and efficient. I have wanted to work with my hands for as long as I can remember, so my mother would set up a miniature studio for me right next to hers wherever we lived. I just always assumed that I would go into the arts in one way or another.

Quilt Pattern 1

I grew up thinking that the only serious arts were painting or sculpting, but when I moved from Massachusetts to California in 1975 as a senior in high school, my possibilities just exploded. I was fortunate to be here during the heyday of the fiber movement in the mid to late '70s. The diversity of cultures as well as the Pacific Rim influences filled me with all sorts of ideas and made me feel as though I could do anything.

In college I explored all the art forms that they offered: jewelry, sculpture, and ceramics. Then, as a graduating senior, I stumbled upon the textile department. It was literally like a light bulb went off. It was really exciting! This is when I discovered the Japanese process of dying fabric, Arashi-Shibori. It is a traditional technique used in kimono design. A width of cotton fabric about 12 inches wide is wrapped around a highly polished and slightly tapered pole that's about the size of a telephone pole. Then it is secured with thread or string; it's a two-person job. The fabric is twisted and compressed onto the pole to create tiny little pleats until the entire pole is filled and then dyed in a vat of indigo. "Arashi-Shibori" translates to "storm," because the original results often looked like sheets of wind and rain falling across the surface of the fabric.

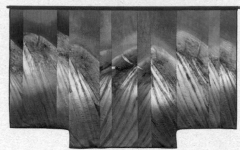

Originally, my personal approach to it was using wine bottles rather than a large log, but I've since switched to a heavy-duty plastic plumbing pipe called ABS. I import dyes from Japan that need to be boiled, and the ABS doesn't melt. ABS also has just the right amount of surface area. I have three specific processes: dyeing, collage (which consists of cutting the fabric, creating the juxtaposition of the colors, and creating the composition), and then finally refining the composition through quilting.

My work has always been influenced by the beauty of nature: reflections on waterfalls, tumultuous flowing rivers, deep canyons, freshwater marshes, tall towering reeds and grasses, and even the colors the sky creates from weather — one minute it's black, dark, and stormy, and the next minute the sun is shining brilliantly and scattering diamonds across an open field. My last series was subtle and somber with vertical lines. The new pieces I am working on are very active — the Shibori cascades with movement. Shibori never fails to amaze me — it's a surprise every time I unwrap a length of fabric.

Quilt Pattern 2

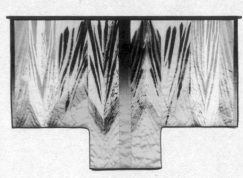

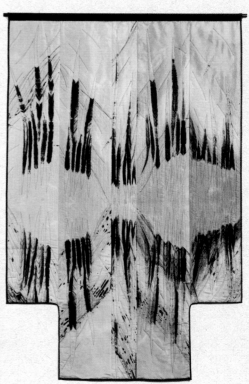

I also give a great deal of my time to volunteer work. I've been very committed and passionate about it. I was president of the Studio Art Quilt Associates, and I volunteer for numerous arts organizations. I just juried Quilt National and have a piece traveling with that exhibition, although most of my work is represented by The Jane Sauer Gallery in Santa Fe, New Mexico. I am presently working on a large commission for a medical center and have been offered my first solo museum show, which is very exciting. At this time I am looking forward to focusing my energies in the studio and really pushing the Shibori to see where I can go with it. It's been more than 30 years now, and I'm still finding new things to do with this technique.

To learn more about Judith Content, visit jsauergallery.com

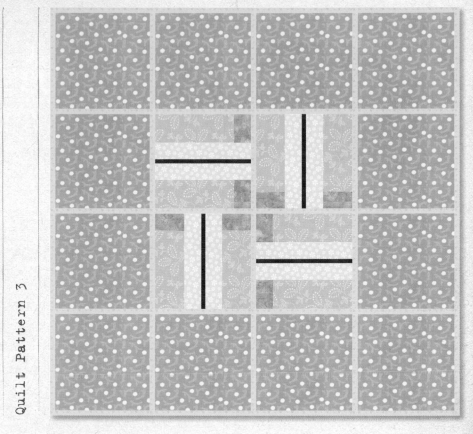

Quilt Pattern 3

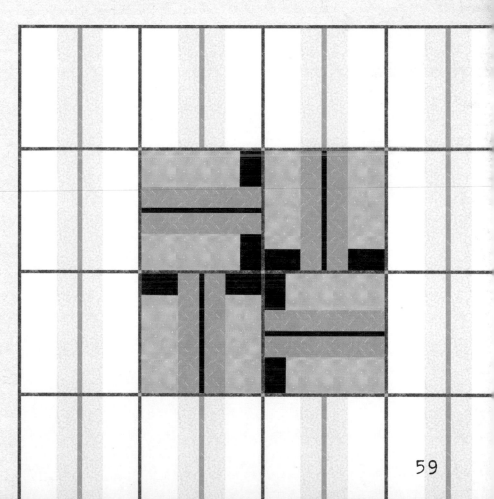

Quilt Pattern 4

Hoodie Crescent

New Jersey graphics artist, Hoodie Crescent, has always been enamored with everything textile. From the time she was a little girl growing up in Japan, one thing has been constant — her love of fabric. Destined to work within the industry, she uses all aspects of her creativity to design a beautiful print. And while her interests are varied: poet, illustrator, artist, designer, and quilter, she always remains true to her original muse.

In the 1960s, I was a young girl living in Japan. During that time period, most housewives were not only homemakers but crafters too. They really did it all, and my mother was no exception. She made my school clothes from the same fabrics she had used to create her own wardrobe. She always added a special little touch, like handmade appliqués or beautiful embroidered designs. She even knitted all of my sweaters and scarves by hand. I remember one year I had a piano recital, and she took me to a fabric store to purchase the cloth for a new dress. I was so excited about each and every step of the sewing process and couldn't wait for the day when I finally got to wear it. I was more excited about creating the dress than the recital itself. It was such a wonderful memory that still sticks with me today.

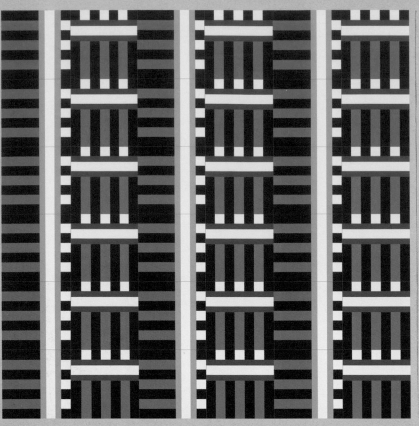

Quilt Pattern 1

I became so interested in textiles that I decided to take home economics classes in high school. I wanted to absorb as much as I could about sewing, knitting, crochet, and embroidery. My mother helped me with my home assignments, and I have the most amazing memories of that time spent with her. It really served to create a strong bond between us. I was so taken with fabrics and every aspect of how they were created that I majored in graphic design and went to work in the textile industry right after graduating. I specialized in home furnishings, bedding, and wallpaper design, and I worked for international companies in USA, Canada and Australia. I was also doing graphic design and illustrations for a monthly magazine.

I used to keep the strike-offs from the textile company I worked for, which were mostly cotton. I would double up the fabric, framing the particular motif I wanted to emphasize, cut it into a shape, stuff it, and sew the "puff" closed. I would then mount these puffy balls of fabric onto a canvas frame and paint them with colorful acrylics. I even did several art shows featuring these creations.

In 1993 I moved from Japan to the U.S. and worked as a freelance designer for Hi Fashion and Timeless Treasures Fabrics. All the while I was still creating my own canvas art and was invited to be in my first show in New York. I actually purchased my first sewing machine here in the U.S. that I used to create my canvas work.

Quilt Pattern 2

In the late '90s there was a lot of changes in my life. My son was born and I became a single mother. It was the beginning of a new phase for me. I stayed really busy and started to work very closely with Kathy Miller when she was a stylist for Timeless Treasures. As we headed into the millennium, my interests turned to 100-percent cotton fabric and, moreover, I discovered The International Quilt Market. It was a whole new world. I started to make little projects like the ones my mother and I had worked on together, as well as aprons, bags, and other small goods using the fabrics that I designed. My sewing life started up again! I gradually began learning all I could about the quilting world. I instinctively knew I had finally found my place. I was home.

Quilt Pattern 4

I love creating and entering my quilts in shows. It's extremely rewarding and fulfilling to work and play among all of my quilter friends in the industry. Currently I am an art director for Newcastle Fabrics and the head textile designer for Newcastle Studio. Look for the Hoodie Crescent licensed line for Newcastle Fabrics coming soon. This year marks my 12th time to attend the International Quilt Market, and I look forward to many, many more.

To learn more about Hoodie Crescent, visit hoodiescollection.com, hoodiescollection.blogspot.com, newfabs.com, *and* inasewingmood.com.

Favorite Quote

"The purpose of art is washing the dust of daily life off our souls."
– Pablo Picasso

Tina Givens

12" x 12" QUILT BLOCK DESIGN

Tina Givens spent her childhood in Southern Africa and now resides in North Carolina with her family. Tina is a creative soul and thoroughly follows her creative path. Working with watercolors, inks, papers, and textiles, she designs an array of products including textiles, apparel, jewelry, gift products, and stationery. Maintaining a separation between the commercial side of her art and products and finding herself through her own artistic exploration is a balance she strives to maintain each day.

I grew up in Southern Africa throughout the '60s and '70s; we were a multicultural family wrapped in a soulful African environment. I had a somewhat normal childhood, believe it or not, and I lived in the sewing room. Before the sewing machine, I hand-stitched my dolls' clothes and accessories and progressed to making my own clothes. Mom taught me as I went along. Both my grandmothers could sew, and one even had a dress shop before I came along. So, sewing was part of our life.

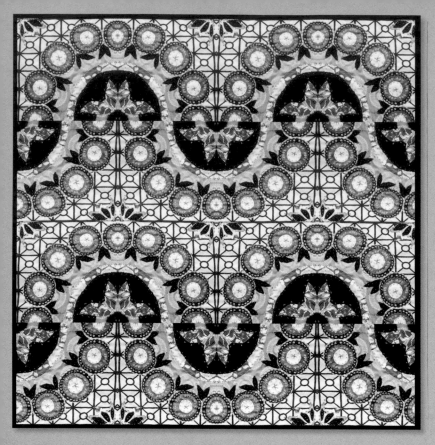

Quilt Pattern 1

Quilt Pattern 2

Quilting was not a common craft in Southern Africa. Africa was all about weaving, beadwork, and sculpture ... I think the English brought the sewing room into the mix. It was only after moving to Northern Africa that I learned to appreciate the art of piecework — I was amazed by the nimble fingers that hand-stitched the quilts through layers of lusciousness!

My first real experience with the world of quilting occurred when I received a wonderful invitation to design for, at the time, relatively new company. It was owned by an old and familiar name — as a child and young adult I used this company's thread in all of my sewing projects. A little overwhelmed yet extremely excited, I visited my first International Quilt Market for the very first time. I met with amazing quilt designers, textile artists, and a whole world I did not know! Painting and designing on paper was an easy process for me, but painting for fabric? That was intimidating and took me a whole year to work up the courage to try. With much patience and encouragement, my mentors and friends and other designers led me by the hand. I spent time studying a handful of amazing designers and finally came out with my first fabric collection.

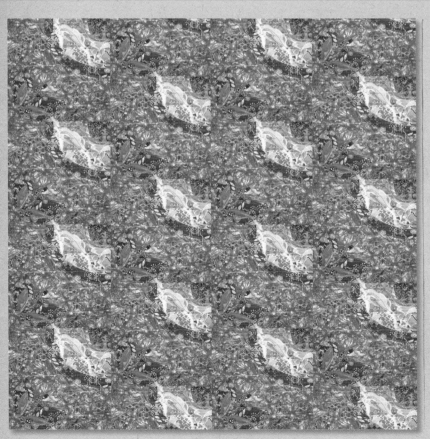

Quilt Pattern 3

Quilt Pattern 4

"An essential aspect of creativity is not being afraid to fail."
– Edwin Land

It was not until much later that I realized my textiles and art had this tribal, multicultural influence. My work was also inspired by turn of the century designers like William Morris, and midcentury eclectic designers like Rose Cumming, who was the queen of chintz and unusual color combinations. Look closely at my work, and you will see this mixture. Inject a little out-of-the-ordinary inspiration, and you'll find what drives my textiles and quilts.

Quilting is a road for me. I have not refined my quilting style but continue to walk down the path, turning a corner every now and then. The end quilt is usually in mind before I design the fabrics, which can come out a little different than expected. When I have the finished fabrics in my hands, I return to the original quilt I had in mind, and it always adapts.

Showing off the fabric is a condition of my quilts, because I intend to share them with you in addition to how I mix the colors. I am getting into more appliqué these days, along with hand-stitching and fun ways to fussy-cut my fabrics. I love having quilts around the house and offering them as gifts to special people. It really is a joy!

To learn more about Tina Givens, visit tinagivens.com, cidpear.com, *and* tinagivenscouture.com.

Heather Grant

A true modernist at heart from Austin, Texas, Heather Grant's real passion is pushing the modern quilt movement forward. Through her popular blog and website, she has been a positive force and instrumental in gathering like-minded artists together, creating a vibrant and thriving community of modern-day quilters.

My mother, grandmother, and great-grandmother were all quilters, and so quilting has always had a special lure for me. I made my first quilt when I was 20. At the time, I wasn't energized about the traditional designs of quilts, but I really loved the craft itself and very much enjoyed the whole process of making a quilt. I was just starting to come into my own, establishing my taste, and found I was especially attracted to midcentury design. I began collecting midcentury modern style furniture. As my appreciation for design developed, I found myself walking away from quilting.

ONLY
ROBINSON CRUSOE
COULD HAVE
EVERYTHING
DONE BY FRIDAY

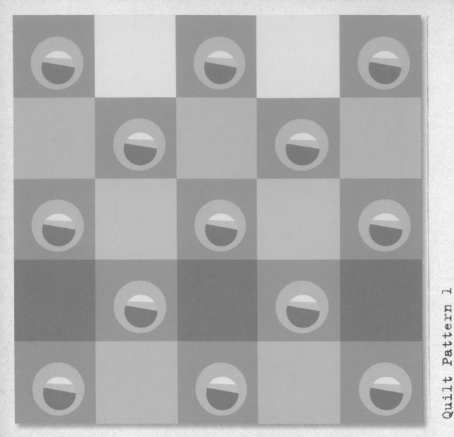

Quilt Pattern 1

In the mid '90s, I was searching for something that interested me. I found Denyse Schmidt's work, and it was truly inspiring. This was a defining moment — I realized that this was the direction I wanted to go, and it helped me resolve the conflict I was having between quilting and style. In 2001 I was working for a book wholesaler called Baker & Taylor in the buying department. It was just happenstance that I ran across Yoshiko Jinzenji's book titled "Quilt Artistry." It was another step forward and brought me closer to where I wanted to be regarding quilting. At this time, modern quilting was not even on the radar; the Internet was just emerging from its tech base. There wasn't any good fabric available on the market yet! In 2005 I discovered two books that would highly influence me and impact my future: "Denyse Schmidt Quilts" by Denyse Schmidt, and "The Modern Quilt Workshop" by Weeks Ringle and Bill Kerr.

I began making modern quilts and posted photos of a couple of them on the Flickr forum group, Fresh Modern Quilts, which was just starting to become a central location for all modern quilters. It was really the first online centralized social media venue. As we began talking with each other and discovering each other's blogs, I finally felt like I was home. Through those blogs I discovered Alissa Haight Carlton and Latifah Saafir, founders of the Modern Quilt Guild in Los Angeles. Like a lot of other people, I was a bit jealous — they had their own guild and I didn't! When I contacted Alissa, she encouraged me to start my own guild, so I started the one in Austin, Texas. By creating The Modern Quilt Guild here, we were finally able to meet one another in person. At the first meeting we had five people, and it grew exponentially from there. For a while I concentrated on my own work, but I found it hard to be creative all of the time. Besides, I get way more excited seeing other people's work! I quickly realized that what I really wanted was to feature the work of others. I had found my niche, and it felt right.

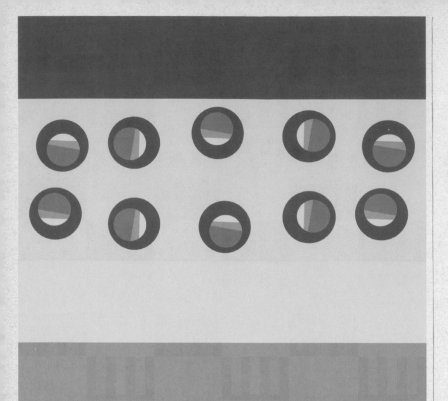

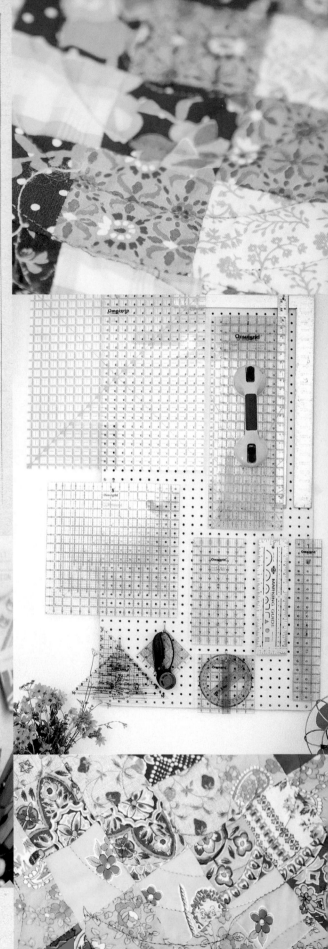

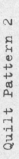

Quilt Pattern 2

ONLY
ROBINSON CRUSOE
COULD HAVE
EVERYTHING
DONE BY FRIDAY

Quilt Pattern 3

Favorite Quote

"I don't see the feathers in the wings, I just count the wings."
– Charley Harper

Presently, I am working with Alissa and focusing on strengthening the Modern Quilt Guild to provide more educational opportunities, which I think will help the craft to grow overall. I am also the director of marketing and programming for QuiltCon, which will take place every other year. I am inspired every day by quilts and feel that by getting together and sharing, whether you are a modernist or traditionalist, we can encourage, support, and inspire each other. I do enjoy creating but am passionate about featuring other artists' work; it's a real pleasure to focus the spotlight where it is deserved. My mission is to bring all modern quilters to the forefront.

To learn more about Heather Grant, *visit* themodernquiltguild.com *and* moderndayquilts.tumblr.com.

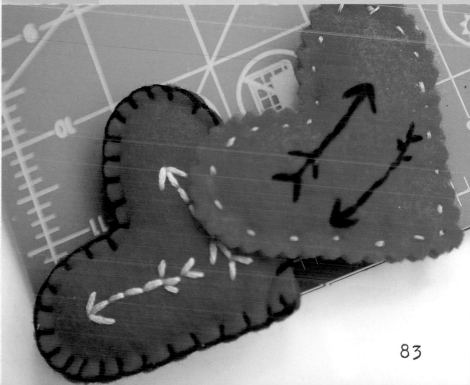

83

The Modern Quilt Guild presented their inaugural convention and quilt show, QuiltCon, from February 21–24, 2013. The idea for the show came about after the Modern Quilt Guild rapidly grew to more than 150 guilds all over the world. In a desire to hold an event that would bring the spread out members together, QuiltCon was born!

When QuiltCon was just an idea, a Twitter conversation about the need for a modern quilt show led Alissa Haight Carlton, The Modern Quilt Guild's executive director, to connect with Heather Grant. Heather's amazing event planning and marketing knowledge led her to join the Modern Quilt Guild as its director of marketing and programming. She quickly started working to turn QuiltCon into a reality. With months and months of incredibly hard work, Heather cranked out an amazing event.

However, she certainly didn't do it alone! The amazing staff and volunteers for the show were so enthusiastic and worked unbelievably hard. They are a perfect example of how the community of modern quilters, who often just know each other through the Internet, can come together to turn an online world into a thriving and vibrant community filled with friendships and inspiration.

As the show was gearing up for its debut, its size and scope gradually grew until it turned into the large-scale event it was. With over 6,400 attendees, the show was definitely a success. QuiltCon featured a wonderful modern quilt show with over 200 hanging quilts, loads of hands-on workshops, and four full days of lectures. The show additionally had a vendor hall that provided great shopping for the modern quilter. The positive energy in the air was palpable, and there's huge excitement about what's to come for the modern quilting community.

QuiltCon will happen all over again in 2015 and is certain to be even bigger and better than the first time around!

To learn more about QuiltCon, visit quiltcon.com.

Alissa Haight Carlton

Alissa Haight Carlton lives in Los Angeles, California, and is the co-founder and executive director of the Modern Quilt Guild. She has written two books: "Modern Minimal: 20 Bold and Graphic Quilts," and "Block Party: The Modern Quilting Bee," which she co-authored. When not working in the modern quilting world, she casts reality shows, including many recent seasons of "Project Runway."

The Internet led me to my passion for modern quilting. Most people have a grandmother who quilted, or they frequented their local quilt shop and took a class … not me. For me it was all about Flickr and blogs. I found Flickr in late 2007 while searching for a place to house my knitting photos. There I found the first photos I'd seen of modern quilts. They called to me like nothing else ever had before. I had to make a quilt, I just had to. I grew up crafty and had a sewing machine, so I wasn't scared to just give it a shot. I bought the book, "Denyse Schmidt Quilts," and dove in. I was instantly in love with the craft. At first I made many, many horrible quilts, but I loved every single one at the time I made it. Slowly my quilts started to become less horrible. I started to look at them with a different eye and think through my designs in a more deliberate way. My quilting grew and improved.

Quilt Pattern 1

Quilt Pattern 2

"Creativity is allowing yourself to make mistakes. Art is knowing which ones to keep."
— Scott Adams

From the start, I consciously pushed myself to grow and develop my work. This is something that I know has benefited me. I almost never make the same quilt twice, but I do explore the same design elements. With each quilt I make, I take one small step along the path I'm on. I try not to look too far down the path and ask big questions; rather I just look to make the next quilt and trust that each one will lead me a little further along the path. When I stop and look back at my past work, the quilts slowly transform in design, focus, and color choices as I gradually hone my voice, quilt by quilt.

There's another aspect to my quilting journey that I can't ignore: my community of modern quilters. Just like the quilts themselves, the community has played a very transformative role in my life. The two have grown simultaneously and driven each other along the way. What this community, and being a part of it, has done for me has been wonderful.

It was through an online virtual quilting bee that the idea of my first book came. Co-written with Kristen Lejnieks, "Block Party: The Modern Quilting Bee" came out in 2011 and featured quilts that were collaboratively made by 12 modern quilters who met online. My more recent book, "Modern Minimal: 20 Bold and Graphic Quilts," followed soon after. This book reflects the quieter and simpler direction that my quilt designs have taken in the past two or three years.

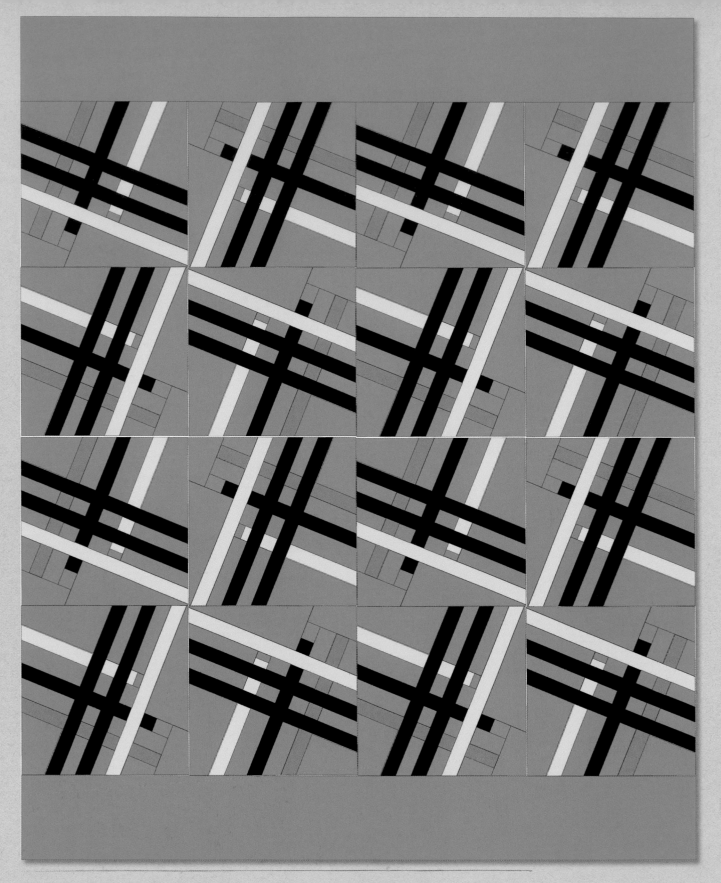

Quilt Pattern 3

The largest way that community has played a huge role in my quilting journey is through the Modern Quilt Guild. In October of 2009, I co-founded the Los Angeles Modern Quilt Guild, and in doing so, the Modern Quilt Guild was founded. At that first meeting of 20 people, we never anticipated that in less than four years, the Modern Quilt Guild would grow to over 150 guilds or that we would hold our first convention, QuiltCon, with over 6,400 attendees. The vibrancy and excitement that was palpable in the air at QuiltCon is what drives me to keep working at the organization, but it's also what makes me want to get started on each new quilt. If I can put one ounce of the positive energy that the community has into my quilting, I know that I'll be going strong for a long time!

To learn more about Alissa Haight Carlton, visit handmadebyalissa.com.

Quilt Pattern 4

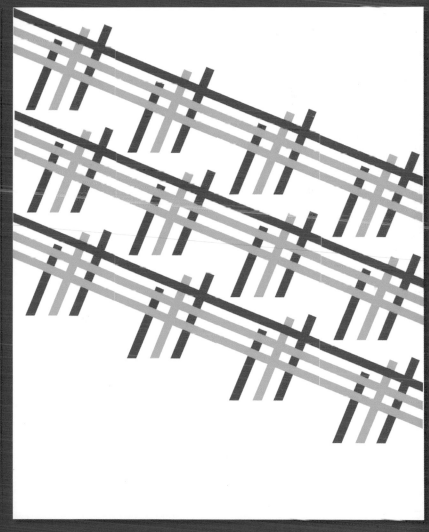

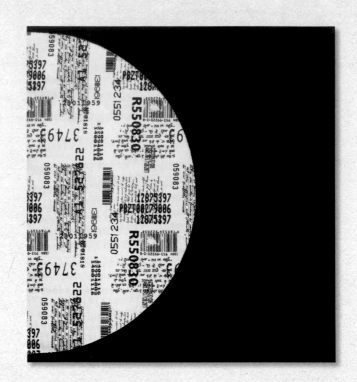

Brigitte Heitland

Brigitte Heitland lives in the lovely town of Werther in north-central Germany and is the founder and owner of Zen Chic, a quilt and textile design studio. Germany doesn't really have much of a quilting tradition, but Brigitte and a few other pioneering women have begun to change that. Once she discovered the world of quilting, it became a passion that transformed her life — perhaps it will change other lives as well.

When I enter my studio, I feel like I have to pinch myself. It seems like only yesterday that this lovely space was the bedroom of my teenage son, with blue and white walls, soccer paraphernalia, and toys and socks on the floor. Now the walls are awash with the palest shade of lavender, set off by vibrant orange and pink circles that bubble up like bright ideas. "Welcome," the room will whisper, and sometimes nudge, "Come on in and create something beautiful!" And indeed, this is now blessedly and miraculously my daily work — to step into this room and create something beautiful.

DON'T BE AFRAID
TO FAIL.
BE AFRAID
NOT TO TRY

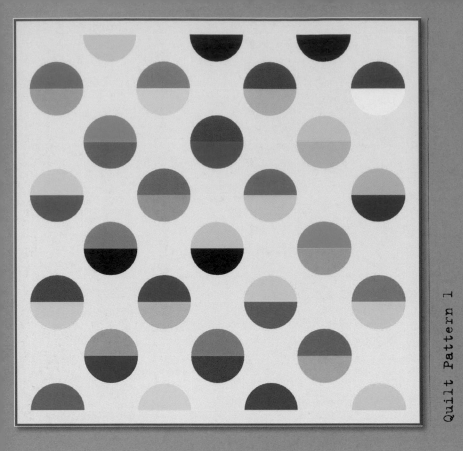

Everything in this space is well-appointed: There is a large island where I measure, cut, and package my fabrics; a computer desk where I design my fabrics and run my online business; a floor-to-ceiling shelving system where all my supplies are stored; and a cozy corner where I can put my feet up when I get tired of all the work and hit a low spot (usually at about 2 o'clock in the afternoon).

Naturally, this space with all its beautiful and functional features did not come together overnight. It evolved alongside my own life as I transitioned from hobby quilter to online store owner and finally to fabric designer. And yet, looking back I can see that some aspects of my current life have been foreshadowed all along.

Even though I am a newcomer to the world of quilts, I have been sewing since I was 6 years old when my grandmother showed me how to use her Pfaff sewing machine. And since I was a teenager, I had this dream that one day I would open up a craft store and sell some very special yarns. But I was young, and it seemed more like a dream than a real way of making a living. So I did what everyone else in my family did: I went to a university and studied, first interior design and then textile design.

And then life happened, children happened, and my dream faded into the background. I began to work as an accountant to provide for my three children, but I never stopped sewing, knitting, and creating. And then one day I stepped into a bookstore and came across a quilting book with fabrics by Kaffe Fassett. And that was it! I knew I had to learn to quilt.

Quilt Pattern 3

From there things happened pretty fast, although not without some detours and setbacks. Suddenly I needed fabrics, lots of fabrics, and before I knew it I had started a little online business buying and selling fabrics. And then I just had to have a long-arm quilting machine, and so I added a long-arm quilting service to my business. And then came the day when I just needed to create my own fabrics. When I took them to a quilt market in the States, Moda saw what I was doing and signed me up. By then it was clear that I had found my calling. With the support and encouragement of my family, I quit my accounting job to concentrate full time on quilting and fabric design.

"Never give up on a dream just because of the time it will take to accomplish it. The time will pass anyway."

– Earl Nightingale

To have the time and space to create my own designs is wonderful, but to find international recognition for my work is beyond what I had imagined. And so, at long last, my dream has come true, not in the way I had pictured it as a young girl, but in a much better and more satisfying way. It took a lot of hard work and a great deal of courage, and some days I fall into bed completely exhausted, but I will always be glad that I followed my heart.

To learn more about Brigitte Heitland, visit farbstoff-bridge.blogspot.com *and* brigitteheitland.de.

Quilt Pattern 4

Lori Holt

12" x 12" QUILT BLOCK DESIGN

Lori Holt lives a happy and creative life in Riverton, Utah, where she is surrounded by the beautiful Wasatch Mountains. She blogs under the name, Bee in my Bonnet, which is also the name of her pattern and design company that she established in 1994. Lori designs her own fabric and currently has six collections. She has recently launched her own quilting ruler/template line. Both her fabric and rulers are produced by Riley Blake Designs. On most days, you can find Lori in her studio playing with fabric and working on her next creation.

I'm a small-town girl who grew up on a farm, and so I spent my happy-go-lucky childhood playing in the sunshine, riding on tractors, and climbing trees. The middle child of a large family, I spent my childhood closely surrounded by grandparents, uncles, aunts, and cousins.

I learned that I was creative at a young age. I was inspired by the color and style of all things around me, and I remember studying the pattern in the fabrics of the double wedding ring quilt that my great-grandmother made. I was fascinated with each tiny piece and would try to find a match to each one in the quilt.

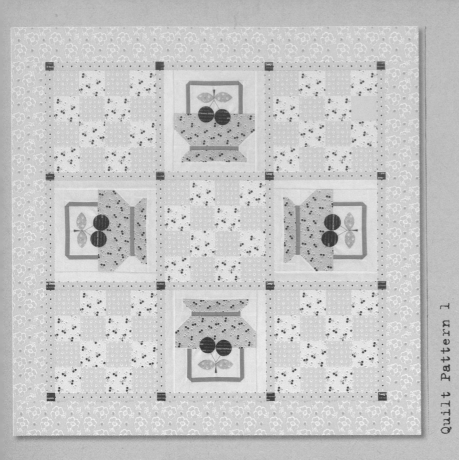

It seemed that we were always making something at our house, and I was content to be immersed in all things domestic. Because my mother sewed most of our clothes, I always had fabric, thread, and buttons close at hand. And so as a girl, I spent many hours designing and sewing clothes for my dolls and making gifts for family and friends. Back then, I loved to sew things for the kitchen like aprons and hot pads, and I still love to sew those things today. My mother and grandmothers thought it was important that my sisters and I learn to sew, and Mom has always said that I was "practically born with a needle in my hand."

I did grow up in a quilting family. It seems there was always a quilt on the frames for a wedding, or a baby, or just because! My earliest memories consist of sitting underneath those frames, threading needles for my grandma and great-aunts until I eventually grew old enough to make stitches of my own.

I also learned how to crochet and embroider at a young age. My deep love of all needle art comes from the early influence of my grandmothers, who were my very first teachers. I cannot remember a time when I did not have a current sewing project. When it was my turn to herd the sheep, I would take my embroidery with me for the afternoon until it was time to bring the sheep back to the pasture. I even brought my sewing with me to school. And as a teenager, I loved to sew decorations for my room. As I grew older, my sisters and I would sew a lot of our own clothes together. We had so many cute dresses and skirts!

Quilt Pattern 2

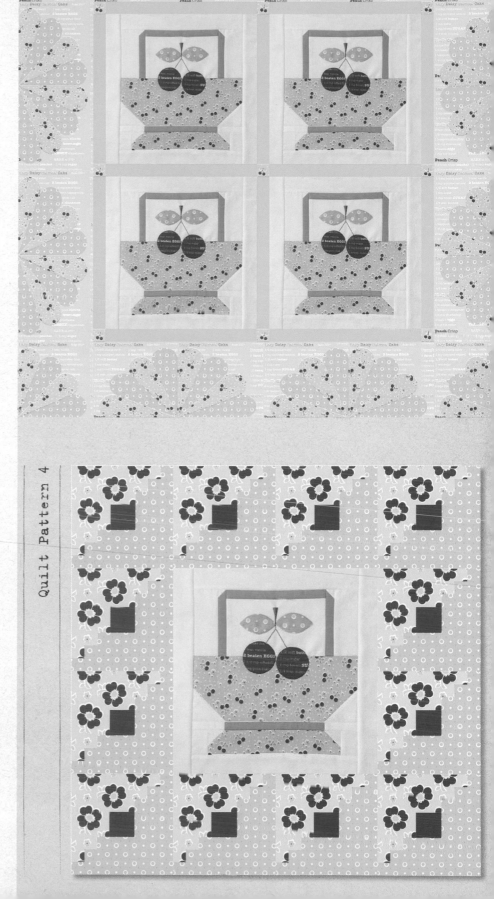

When I was 15, I designed and made my very first quilt on my own. I remember drawing the design using a mechanical pencil on graph paper. I had borrowed my supplies from my dad's desk; he was a mechanical engineer. I still use these same basic tools to design all of my quilts.

I realize now that growing up immersed in such a creative life was unusual, but back then it was just normal to me and made for a very happy and productive experience. I am now married to my best friend and childhood sweetheart, and together we have three creative, intelligent children as well as a 4-year-old granddaughter. I try to teach my children and students to be creative every day. I find joy in using my creativity to make beautiful things on a daily basis. I draw inspiration for my designs from the beauty of the earth, from the love of God, and from all things vintage. I have a deep love for vintage … I know that this comes from my many wonderful family memories.

I sew, draw, create, decorate, and redecorate on a daily basis. I think of myself as the luckiest girl in the world because I get to do what I love every day. I feel blessed to be able to live a creative life. My wish is that my designs in both patterns and fabric will inspire others to create. I also wish they will instill the desire to pass down the valuable lessons of days gone by that have been taught to us by our mothers and grandmothers.

To learn more about Lori Holt, visit beeinmybonnetco.blogspot.com.

Quilt Pattern 4

Leslie Tucker Jenison

12" x 12" QUILT BLOCK DESIGN

Leslie Tucker Jenison is an award-winning mixed-media artist from San Antonio, Texas. Dyes and paints are integral components of her surface design work, which has been shown internationally and featured in numerous publications. Leslie is a member of many professional artist organizations, serves on the board of the Quilt Alliance, and is one half of the curating-teaching duo, Dinner at Eight Artists. Leslie enjoys photography, reading, gardening, and traveling; and she is a private pilot with multi-engine and instrument ratings. Leslie is married and has three daughters, all artists.

Art has been a part of my story since childhood. My parents encouraged any and all artistic pursuits that captured my fancy. I learned to sew on an 1890s-era Singer treadle machine that we found at a garage sale in the early '60s for $5. My paternal grandmother, Maude Tucker, was a huge influence on me as a child. As a seamstress in a tiny north-central Kansas town, she was constantly working on a garment or quilt when I visited. A quilt could always be found stretched across a frame in an upstairs bedroom. Stitchery was a way of life for her — a source of income and pleasure.

Quilt Pattern 1

I re-discovered my love of textiles as artful expression soon after finishing nursing school while working as an RN in labor and delivery. I was intrigued by a nurse colleague who worked on quilts before she began her shift on the unit. Eventually, she took me under her wing and encouraged me to explore the world of quilt making.

I was fortunate to find Virginia Robertson as my first quilting teacher. At that time, Virginia operated a small industry out of her home where she created items for a high-end catalog and taught small classes. I took my first class in her home and learned how to hand-applique. Soon after, Virginia expanded her business and moved to the site of an old church building in the small town of Overbrook, Kansas, and named it the Osage County Quilt Factory. I drove to a "Block-of-the-Month" class every month, learning how to create all sorts of pieced and appliquéd styles. This became the backbone of my skill set for almost all of the pieced work I create, even today. Having these basic skills has enabled me to expand and explore a much wider variety of styles.

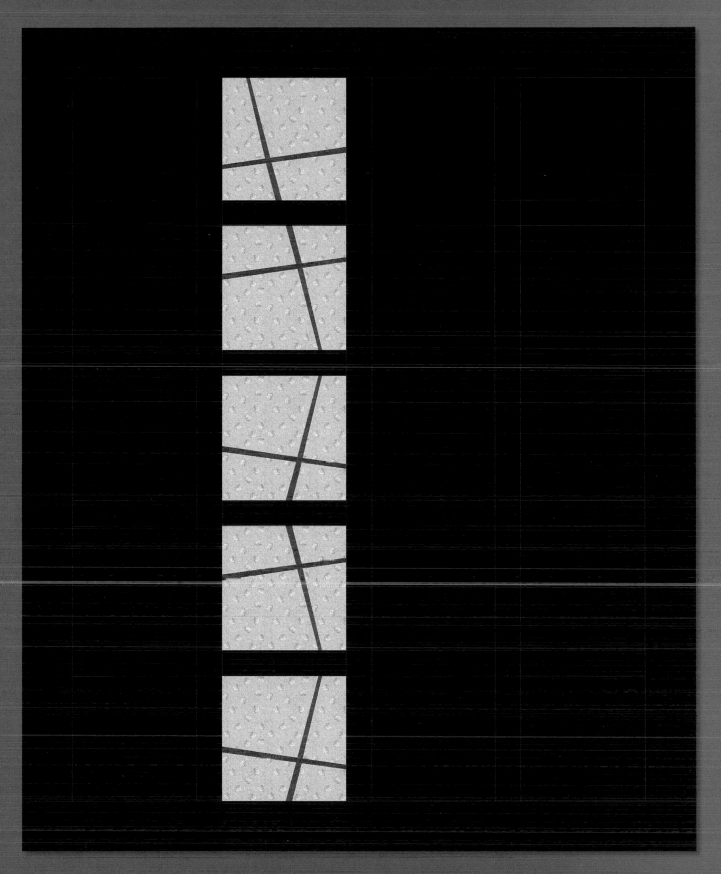

Quilt Pattern 2

My personal life grew: I fell in love and married a wonderful human being, became a mother, and continued working in the field of women's health. I found time for creativity when I could, but the demands of raising three daughters took priority for many years, leaving minimal time for artwork. My artistic life was placed on the back burner.

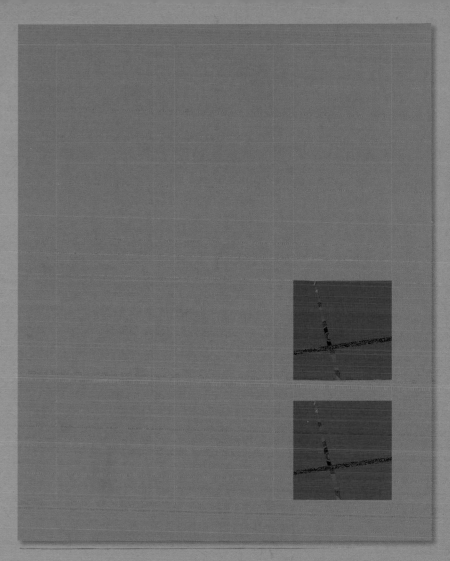

Quilt Pattern 3

In the early '90s, Debra Lunn exposed me to hand-dyed cloth at a quilt show in Kansas City. Little did I know that a few years later I would land in a hot bed of dyeing and surface design activity that would radically change my work. My husband relocated his company to San Antonio, Texas, in 1997. Although I was sad to leave my hometown, I looked forward to a new city and all the possibilities that new beginnings offer.

I began a love affair with my new city by juggling the Master Gardener program, painting, and my daughters' school and sports events. I discovered the work of Jane Dunnewold and the art cloth movement soon after. Family responsibilities changed, my children grew up, and my time became my own again. And so, I dove into my art. I returned to textiles and quilting, finding surface design (dyeing and mark-making on cloth and paper) to be the alchemy for my personal artistic expression. I began showing my work in 2002.

"Life is not a dress rehearsal."
– Rose Tremain

After my youngest daughter left for college, I returned to my other passions, teaching and writing. Although I limit my teaching in order to ensure enough studio time, I love the workshop environment and exchange of ideas. I co-curate and frequently teach with my partner in crime, Jamie Fingal, as one-half of Dinner at Eight Artists. Our juried invitational exhibitions have traveled to major quilt shows in the U.S. and Europe. For me, as an artist, the journey is the destination. I savor every single moment of it!

To learn more about Leslie Tucker Jenison, visit leslietuckerjenison.blogspot.com *and* leslietuckerjenison.com.

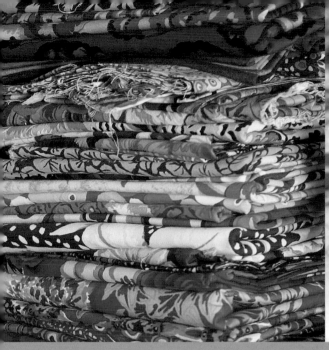

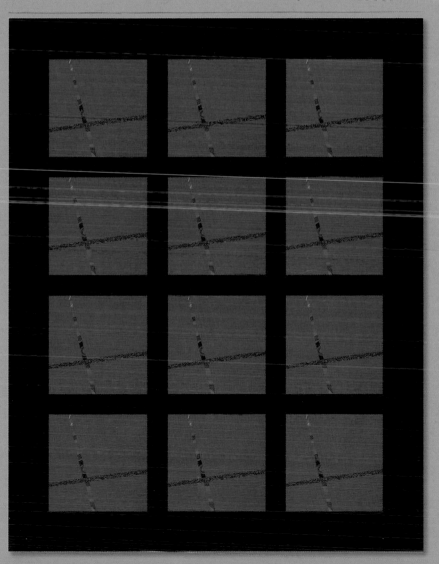

Quilt Pattern 4

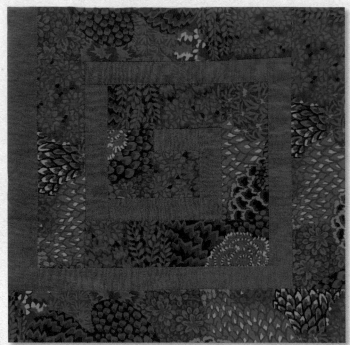

Liza Prior Lucy
& Kaffe Fassett

Located in New Hope, Pennsylvania, Liza Prior Lucy was destined to work with textiles. She considers herself to be a 21st century rag peddler. Her mother and grandmother made socks for the soldiers during World War II, and her great-great-grandfather came to America as a rag peddler. Liza collaborates with friend and fellow quilt and fabric designer, celebrated London artist and author, Kaffe Fassett. Fate brought them together to create exquisite, captivating, and gloriously colorful patchwork masterpiece quilts.

I am a quilt maker, an organic gardener, and a mom. As far back as I can remember, I have never been without some kind of fiber running through my hands; fabric has always been a part of my life. I made my first quilt by sewing together 25 bandanas for my boyfriend's waterbed in college.

After college, I went to grad school for a while and then opened up my own needlepoint store in Washington, D.C. I married the waterbed boy, but when he suddenly passed away at 30, I decided to close up shop and start over again. I became a knitting yarn sales rep for several companies in New York, New Jersey, and Pennsylvania.

One day I walked into one of my big accounts in New York and saw this beautiful book called "Glorious Knits" by Kaffe Fassett. I had never seen anything so fantastic in my life. It was an absolute revolution — it turned everything I knew about knitting upside down. As fortune would have it, when I got home that night I received a phone call from Ken Bridgewater asked if I would like to work as a representative for his import company. I was going to decline until he told me that the yarn he was importing was from Rowan in Yorkshire ... and they were working with Kaffe Fassett. I immediately said, "Yes!" I went to work for Rowan, and when Kaffe came to America on his first book-signing tour, it was my privilege to take him around my territory. That's how we became friends.

Flash-forward five years. I was remarried to my first husband's best friend and expecting my first child at 38 years old. I decided to make a baby quilt and was simply fascinated by the process and end result. I sent a postcard to Kaffe that read something like this: "Hey there, want to write a quilt book with me?" He wrote back: "Been traveling, finishing up a book called 'Glorious Interiors,' terribly busy, nice to hear from you." That was Kaffe's way of politely saying no. I started to make little quilt patches (pillow-sized pieces based on his knitting) and mailing them to him. Once again, fate stepped in. During this period I was contacted by a woman who was selling a painting of a patchwork quilt by Kaffe Fassett. Needless to say, I bought it.

The next time Kaffe came to the U.S., he saw that I had obtained the painting. He felt it was one of his finest and figured it was a sign from the universe that we should make quilts together. I couldn't have been more pleased! As of now, we have made five hardcover and 15 softcover books together. Kaffe and I, and our friends at Rowan, launched the Rowan Patchwork & Quilting Fabric Company, which was then purchased by Coats and is now called Westminster. We stay on the creative side of things and talk to each other almost daily. It's been really wonderful. We create an annual softcover book and are presently working on the newest edition.

Quilt Pattern 2

KAFFE FASSETT QUILTS
SHOTS AND STRIPES
24 New Projects Made with Shot Cottons and Striped Fabrics

KAFFE FASSETT AND LIZA PRIOR LUCY
photographs by Debbie Patterson

123

I hope that the future brings more collaboration with Kaffe because there is nothing that makes me happier. I have learned so much from him. I consider myself the most fortunate quilt maker on the planet! I still learn from him every day … he learns from me too, though. He knows how to handle a rotary cutter now.

I will never stop making quilts. I have the greatest respect for my materials. I love putting colorful fragments of quilts back together to create a unique pattern. I find every aspect of patchwork quilt making to be entirely and utterly satisfying.

To learn more about Liza Prior Lucy and Kaffe Fassett, visit gloriouscolor.com *and* kaffefassett.com.

Katie Pasquini Masopust

Katie Pasquini Masopust is an artist who lives in Santa Fe, New Mexico, with her husband and three big dogs. She is a quilter, painter, and an author of several books on her design style. Katie finds joy in creating and traveling to teach her techniques all over the world.

12" x 12" QUILT BLOCK DESIGN

I was a painter before I became a quilter. I started drawing and painting when I was a little girl and was encouraged by my wonderful parents. In high school, I chose all my elective classes from the art department. I tried everything from calligraphy and jewelry to printing and painting. I loved oil painting the most.

At the end of my senior year, I moved to the San Francisco Bay Area to care for my terminally ill mother. I took several classes there at the community college. I signed up for an oil painting class and what I thought was an embroidery class. The oil painting class was not very encouraging to such a young student, so I dropped that. The embroidery class turned out to be a quilting class, but the other students were so supportive that I decided to stick with it. I ended up creating several traditional quilts. When my mother and I moved back to Eureka, California, I opened a quilt shop that I ran for almost five years; I taught traditional classes there.

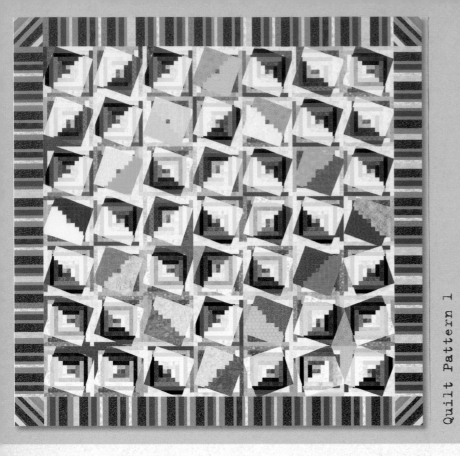

Somewhere in between, I met and married a wonderful man who is very supportive of my work. We moved to Santa Fe, New Mexico, where we set up my beautiful studio right off the living room in the house we helped design. He likes to cook, so the kitchen is right off the living room too. I love Santa Fe's landscape, and we live out of town so I can walk my three dogs in the arroyos and enjoy the scenery without getting into my car. It was here in Santa Fe that we started up Alegre Retreat, an art quilters' getaway. I closed it down after 14 years and moved it to a student's resort in Gateway Colorado — 2013 is our fifth year in the new location.

I then attended a quilt conference where I met Michael James. I took several classes from Michael, and he encouraged me to use my knowledge of making a quilt and my talent as an artist to create my own designs. That's where I took off. I sold my quilt shop and started traveling and teaching my design techniques. My first classes were on mandala designs: designs that radiate from a center with repeating wedges. This class soon became a book, and I was in demand all over the world to teach. I made several mandalas working in a series, even though I didn't realize it at that time. I then moved on to designing three-dimensional quilts on a two-dimensional surface; this too became a book. And this became a pattern for me: I would start a new series, work on it for a few years, teach the techniques to my students, and write a book about it for the finale. This was the way I was making my living. "Isometric Perspectives" followed, then "Fractured Landscape," "Ghost Layers and Color Washes," and "Color and Composition," co-written with Brett Barker. My latest two books are "Design Explorations" and "Inspirations in Design."

Still wanting to give back to the quilting community, my husband and I started up the YEA (Young Emerging Artist) award. Several years ago at Quilt National in Athens, Ohio, I met some wonderful artists who were very young and excited about the medium. They were struggling to raise their families and make their art. We wanted to encourage the young fiber artists to continue with their art, so we decided to give an award of $700 to a Quilt National artist 30 years of age or younger. We all need to encourage the young to make their art.

This has carried over to Alegre Retreat where the Hendricks' (owners of the resort) give a full scholarship to a deserving young artist to enable them to attend the workshops without any monetary hardship. Our first YEA scholarship so impressed another student, Mrs. Chapin, that she sponsors a second YEA scholarship as well. We encourage anyone under the age of 30 to go to our website at alegreretreat.com and apply for the scholarship.

To learn more about Katie Pasquini Masopust, visit katiepm.com.

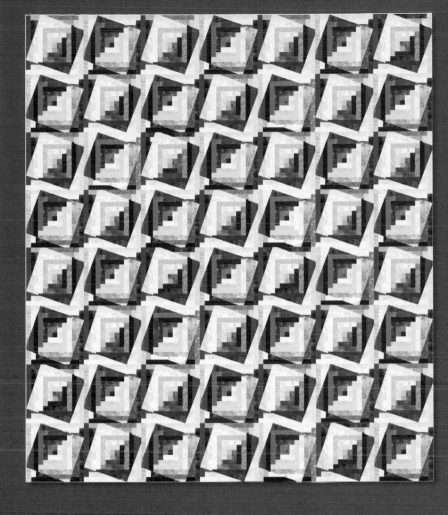

Favorite Quote

"Color gets all the credit while value does all of the work."
– Author Unknown

Kaari Meng

Kaari Meng is the owner of French General, located in Los Angeles, California. The creative idea she started 15 years ago when her daughter Sofia was born gradually grew into her lifestyle business that she runs with her husband, JZ. She additionally creates a line of sewing- inspired paper crafts for Jolee's Boutique; designs quilting fabric for Moda; and designs home decorating fabric, wallpaper, and trim for Fabricut.

Kaari teaches creative workshops in California and takes groups of women to the South of France every year to find their inner French woman. To this day she has written five books. Kaari believes in the power of creative thinking and is thankful every day for the arts and crafts movement that she is a part of.

By the time this book is published, I hope to have made my very first quilt all by myself. You see, I am not a quilter or even much of a sewer for that matter. I am a fabric designer, hoarder, curator, lover, and collector ... but not a quilter. I own many old quilts and many old pieces of quilts. I think of myself as a caretaker of the quilts I own — I take care of them for now and hopefully they will be passed down for years to come. I will travel for days to look at a quilt, to be in the presence of a quilt, and to hear the quilt's story. I am curious who made the quilt, why the quilt was made, where the fabric came from and who eventually, took care of the quilt. My curiosity has led me on a fabric journey that has fulfilled a lifelong dream: to surround myself with beautiful textiles rich in history.

My love affair with quilts began when I started designing quilting fabric for Moda. A knock on the front door at French General has turned into six years of designing beautiful French-inspired fabric for the quilting industry. I spend countless hours at flea markets looking for inspiration to design our next collection of fabric. During the summer, I visit the markets in France and consider it a good day if I find a scrap of 19th century fabric hidden in an old sewing basket. From that one tiny French scrap, a palette, a concept for prints, and a theme emerge. Imagination kicks in and I am dreaming up the latest fabric collection for Moda. My antique textile menagerie is now bursting at the seams, but I continue to add old quilts — they seem to be calling my name.

I have always been attracted to old, tattered, and frayed quilts. When I walk through a flea market, the quilt being used as its dealer's packing blanket or as a flatbed liner is the one I go after. There is something about a worn and discarded piece of fabric that interests me. Dealers normally disregard my request for a price with, "Oh that old thing? Nah, you can't have that. I need that to keep the rain off of my furniture." If it's really falling apart and I can't bear the quilt having one more night in the rain, I persist. Sometimes the price is based on what it will cost for the dealer to replace his tarp, but often there is no price — the dealer won't sell something that has become so useful to him. This is why I love quilts … not only are they beautiful, they are useful too.

"You can't use up creativity. The more you use, the more you have"
– Maya Angelou

Second to finding an old quilt that needs love and care, I look for the quilt that might have a secret second quilt underneath the first. Often used as the filling or batting, a worn out, old quilt can sometimes be found peeking out of the small stitches or seams. A weekend spent picking apart one quilt to get to another is my guilty pleasure. I call it the twofer: getting two quilts for the price of one. But really, the ultimate use of a quilt is giving it new life by sewing a new cover — make do and mend at its best.

Being a part of the quilting community has been a gift. I have learned so much from many talented people who have designed and sewn quilts for all of their lives. I love the colorful, textured history that I have become a part of by designing fabric and patterns for the quilting community.

To learn more about Kaari Meng, visit frenchgeneral.com, frenchgeneral.blogspot.com, the-art-of-craft.com.

Quilt Pattern 3

Quilt Pattern 4

Amanda Murphy

Amanda Murphy is an author, fabric and pattern designer, and quilt artist known for her exuberant use of color and juxtaposition of modern and traditional motifs, patterns, and techniques. A graphic designer by training, Amanda's interests and experiences led her to quilting, an art that marries her passion for design with her enthusiasm for handwork. She markets her own pattern line and designs quilting collections for Blend Fabrics, a subsidiary of Anna Griffin Inc. Amanda is also the author of two books with C&T Publishing — "Modern Holiday" and "Color Essentials."

Like most quilters, I love fabric. The endless array of colors and patterns and the tactile quality of cloth never fail to inspire me. I'm particularly interested in the juxtaposition of modern and traditional motifs. When I'm in the process of designing a new fabric collection, I frequently bounce back and forth between fabric and quilt designs, adjusting color values and scale. Ultimately, I develop a family of designs that can be combined in a myriad of ways. Places like Winterthur, Hillwood, and Williamsburg are inspirational to me, and I am intrigued with the lives of the artists who created the beautiful objects that one sees there.

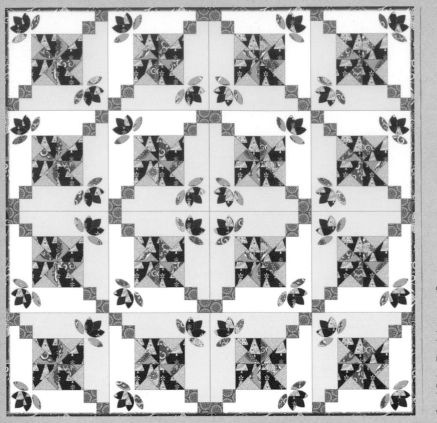

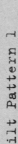

AMANDA AM MURPHY

As artists, I think it is important for quilters to challenge themselves to go beyond their comfort zone and try new techniques or styles. These experimental projects don't have to be on a large scale — pillow tops, table runners, or even fabric postcards are perfect opportunities to try something new. Doing this has led to some of my greatest opportunities in the quilting industry, like my partnerships with Bernina and Brewer/OESD and my books with C&T Publishing.

As a quilt designer, I frequently challenge myself to develop a color palette that I'm comfortable with and then throw a "poison" color into the mix. A lot of times that poison color may not be a personal favorite, but it will add a much-needed kick to the finished piece. (I have a personal abhorrence of the color orange, but it makes frequent appearances in my collections because it is a particularly effective hue in conjunction with my favorite greens and blues.) I also try to take as many classes as I possibly can — you never know when the need might arise to incorporate a particular technique into your work.

Although I was educated as an industrial designer and worked professionally as a graphic designer, I have always been drawn to textile design. Quilting is a great fit for me because I enjoy using both the left and right sides of my brain. I like creating art one day and writing directions the next. My best creative ideas frequently come when I'm focusing on other things, and the wide variety of tasks that I do as a small business owner are a catalyst for this.

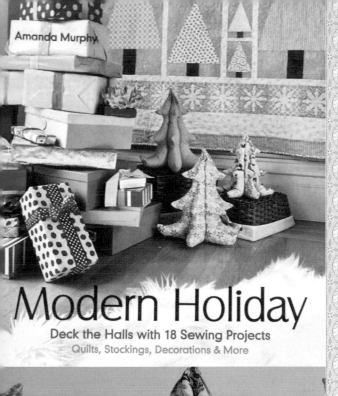

Quilt Pattern 2

147

Favorite Quote

Favorite Quote

"Creativity is allowing yourself to make mistakes. Art is knowing which ones to keep."

– Scott Adams

Quilt Pattern 3

I am fortunate to have a finished space above our garage to store bolts of colorful fabrics, patterns, and books. But if I'm honest, the real work always happens in our front family room, where a revolving assortment of schoolwork, computers, and sewing and art supplies make their appearance. Much of my work is done at night when it's quiet. During the day, there is a constant flurry of activity in our home, which doubles as a business, and it can be quite chaotic at times. We definitely don't have a traditional family room or living room or a picture-perfect house — ours is one of creative chaos. But because of this, our kids know that learning is a lifelong adventure and that it is important not to wait for the perfect time to shoot for your dreams.

Creativity is one of the greatest joys in life — experience it to the fullest. Create as much as you can, even if you only have 15 minutes a day, and help others discover that joy as well. Don't wait for the perfect studio space or time, and enjoy making the things that you love.

To learn more about Amanda Murphy, visit amandamurphydesign.com *and* amandamurphydesign.blogspot.com.

Quilt Pattern 4

Michele Muska

Michele Muska lives in a world of colorful fibers and textiles. Making one-of-a-kind-pieces of fiber and needle-felted jewelry, purses, and quilts is her passion. You may also find her in her beautiful gardens crafting sculptures out of old sinks and copper pipes. Or, you might possibly find her in her little kitchen cooking up a batch of one of her famous soups or pies (well, famous in her family at least).

She is a woman who loves all things creative. Like all of her artwork, Michele strongly believes in working in the moment, and quilting is no different. She enjoys the process of creating as much as the end result. Michele sits on the board of The Quilt Alliance, a non-profit organization that promotes the preservation and culture of quilts and quilt making throughout the world.

I learned to sew by hand before I was 5 years old. My mom and cousins taught me how to make little doll clothes out of felt and dress scraps from my mom's stash. Most mornings when Mom would open my door to wake me up I would already be knitting, painting, drawing or sewing. I just had to create. When Mom let me use her cast-iron Kenmore with a knee pedal, I couldn't have been more excited. It was perfect since my feet didn't reach the ground for a foot pedal. I loved sitting at her machine, located in her bedroom that always felt like a safe haven from my wild brothers. The view of the backyard and garden was peaceful even in the winter months, and the three large windows let the light flood in. The machine had already seen many garments and quilts being made ... first by Aunt Sybil, then by Mom, and now by me.

Viola Rae by Michele Muska

261 Broad Brook Rd · Enfield, CT 06082
email: michele@michelemuska.com · www.michelemuska.com

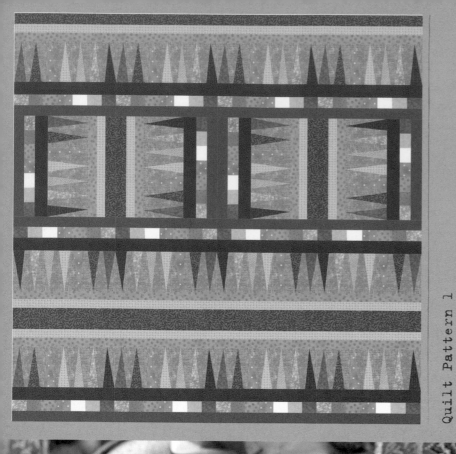

Quilt Pattern 1

Favorite Quote

"Be in love with your life. Every minute of it."
— Jack Kerowac

The first quilt I made was a simple twin-sized nine-patch that I designed out of dress fabrics backed with an old sheet; I used a flannel blanket for the batting that I just took right off my bed. I can vividly remember zigzagging the bright mustard-gold sash down. That quilt lasted for many years. We used it as our picnic blanket when I got married, and we used it in the backyard when my babies first learned to sit up. I can still remember picking the fabrics from the large African basket my mom kept her scraps in; my cousin brought it back for her from his time in the Peace Corps. It seemed so exotic to me, and I dreamed of what life was like so far away as I dug to the bottom for the pieces I needed. All the leftover fabric from my mom's gowns and my party and school dresses were in there, quietly nestled and tumbled together lying in wait.

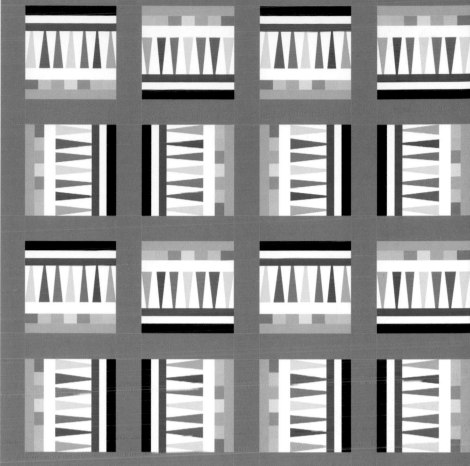

Quilt Pattern 2

It wasn't until I met my husband that I made my second quilt (which we just recently discovered in the blanket closet!). It's a very large green-and-white block quilt (again, made from an old white sheet) with an embroidered center motif of a very abstract floral design. It appears to be a cross between an Eastern European design and prehistoric plant life.

These days I am mostly inspired by color when designing a quilt. The color and fabric usually come first, and the design follows. It's the process of putting things together that intrigues me. I have to say, I am obsessed with the Dresden Plate and wedge though. It was at Paducah almost 10 years ago that my friend, and famous quilter, Darlene Zimmerman, showed me how to use it. I began selecting fabrics while I was there and cut out and pieced the first plates together in a neighboring booth that was selling sewing machines. I spent several years deciding on the fate of those plates. They now float along as abstract lily pads on a wall hanging in my studio. There's about 100 yo-yos, some stuffed and others flat, floating alongside them. All these years later, Darlene keeps telling me, "You know Michele, there are other shapes out there." Of course I know that, and of course I have used them before, but why bother? I'm just not finished with this one yet. So, Darlene started me on the path of using her EZ Dresden tool, and I guess I have her to blame.

155

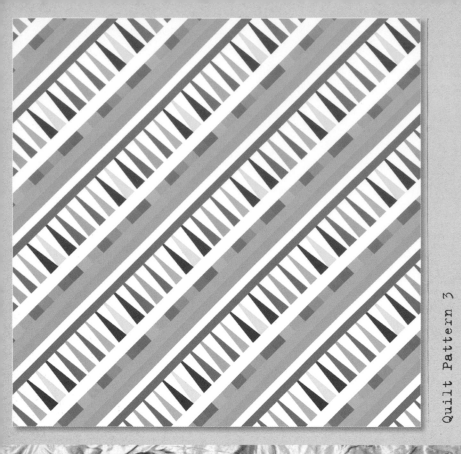

Quilt Pattern 3

I love to use silks and velvets as well as cottons, and I recently made my first queen-sized bed quilt for my husband. It's a bit modern with incredible quilting on it by my friend Shelly Pagliai of Prairie Moon Quilts. My husband Dan says she turned a beautiful quilt into an heirloom! Another first this past year was a collaborative quilt, "The Exquisite Journey," with Frances Holiday Alford, Hoodie Crescent, Victoria Findlay Wolfe, Kathy York, and Leslie Tucker Jenison that was accepted into to the International Quilt Association's Houston show. What a thrill that was for me. We hope to find a home for it that maybe children can enjoy.

More recently I made a little quilt for Baby June Bug, my great-niece, and of course it has Dresden wedges of fun pea green, orange, and brown. So I guess it's only fitting that my quilt block here begins with the Dresden wedge.

To learn more about Michele Muska, visit lolarae.com

Quilt Pattern 4

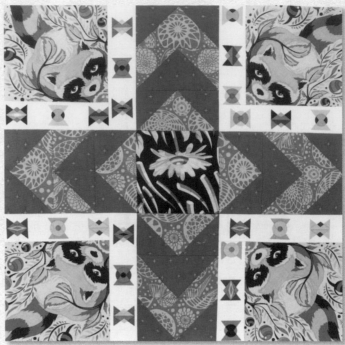

Tula Pink

Tula Pink was born and raised near the sunny shores of Southern California. Though her family and friends worshiped the sun the way most Californians are raised to do, Tula was always more of an indoor kitty, preferring to retreat into the worlds she created in her imagination over the reality of what was gleamed through her eyes alone. Today that creative spark has developed into a craft and lifestyle brand of over a dozen designer fabric collections, quilts, patterns, books, woven ribbons, threads, and more.

I did not come from a long line of quilters or grow up with any great tradition of quilting. My grandmother was an expert shopper and wielded a credit card better than she ever handled a needle and thread. I was a sheep of a different sort. By 12 years old, I had used and, in most cases, abused every art or craft tool that came my way. My grandmother gave me a sewing machine that year for Christmas. I spent the next several months cutting up and reconstructing just about every piece of fabric that my mom's skillfully decorated house had to offer. It didn't take long for my mom to realize that she needed to get me to a fabric store.

Quilt Pattern 1

WHERE WOMEN CREATE—QUILTERS: THEIR QUILTS • THEIR STUDIOS • THEIR STORIES

My first quilt shop was a sea of patterns, lines, shapes, and colors. I was in awe of the possibilities. Combining prints, coordinating colors, and cutting it all up into little pieces to be sewn back together into brilliant new shapes sounded like the best possible way to spend my time, and it still is.

Like any passion, there is always that point when you're so familiar with your materials that nothing satisfies the hunger. I needed more. I needed something that I wasn't finding enough of at my local quilt shops. I needed fabrics that reflected my own lifestyle, so like any good control freak, I decided to make them myself. I designed my first fabric collection and sent it off to a manufacturer for advice, and in two days time I was a fabric designer. With my own fabrics, my quilts were truly my own; they also belonged to everyone else who chose to use them for their projects. This collaboration between myself and everyone who used my fabrics became the ultimate inspiration for future quilts and future fabric collections. This idea of infinite possibilities and anonymous collaborations is the essence of what drives me every day to make new things and explore new ways to draw and sew. The bottom line is that I love it. I love imagining the concept and then seeing how people everywhere interpret that vision and infuse it with their own meaning.

Quilt Pattern 2

Favorite Quote

"They are ill discoverers that think there is no land, when they can see nothing but sea."

— Francis Bacon

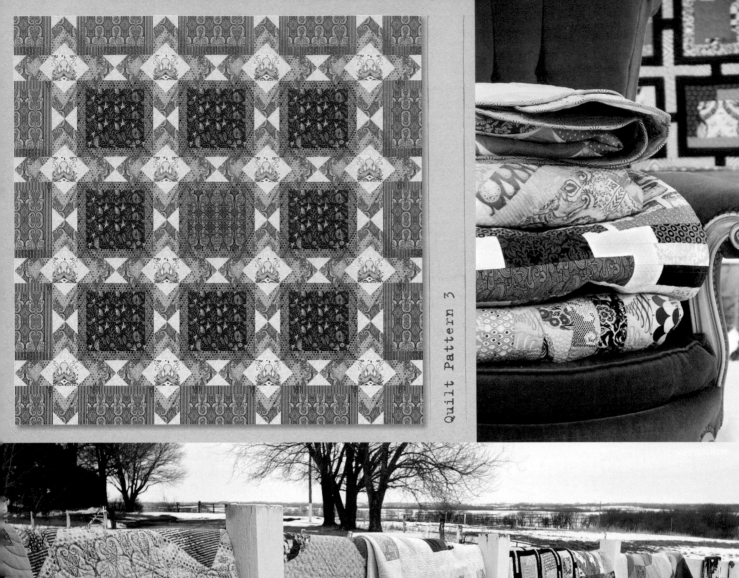

Quilt Pattern 3

My quilts are inspired by the fabrics first. I find the colors and shapes that I want to use, I choose my prints very carefully, and it is only then that I will set out to divide what to make with them. I like to come up with a quilt that will expand the story of the fabrics and add detail or a framework for the fabrics to exist in. I like my patchwork and my prints to coexist. My goal is always to make it seem that one could not fully exist without the other. Sometimes I achieve it, but more often I don't. It's the striving for the goal that makes it exciting and keeps my process fresh.

Quilts are how I communicate. I was drawn to quilting by the beauty of simple patchwork, each shape containing a pattern and another story. Quilts are like a never-ending novel — there is always more to learn, more to see, and more hidden gems to discover. Each quilt, simple or complex, carries with it the story of the quilt maker, the pattern writer, the fabric designer, and the intended recipient. Each part is just as important as any other part. Quilting is a craft steeped in history, and each generation of new quilters bring yet another point of view. It is forever evolving in the hands of its current community. Quilts are art that can be used, and it is this utilitarian nature of quilting that is so fascinating to me.

To learn more about Tula Pink, visit
tulapink.com.

Quilt Pattern 4

Victoria Findlay Wolfe

Victoria Findlay Wolfe is a quilter, artist, author, wife, mother, and fabric designer who is constantly in search of her next creative project. Sewing and quilting from a very young age, she fondly recalls being mesmerized by the stacks of her grandmother's quilts that sat on Victoria's bed on the farm in Minnesota. The process of how to make just about anything is something that drives Victoria's impulse to constantly try new things.

As a child, I was always picking up my mother's scraps to make Barbie clothes, painting winning ceramics at the county fair, and weaving and braiding yarn just to make something new. I guess some things never change. The way my life has turned out, I am still doing that — always trying to make something new. At a very young age, I decided to be an artist, and I never wavered from that ambition.

I was told that if I wanted to be an artist, New York was the place to go. So, I moved to New York to find out who I was and how far I could go. I went on an adventure to find my people! And I can tell you, New York did not disappoint me. I met my husband, and we started our family. I began to sew and quilt to make beautiful things for my daughter, Beatrice. I found textiles to be a quick and easy fix for my creative urges, and from that, my "15 minutes of Play" process was born: I knew I needed at least 15 minutes of "make time" to creatively be happy.

My life took an amazing turn when I found an online community of quilters who shared my interests. I found that I was not alone in being scrap obsessed, cranking out wildly colorful quilts. I found and met other people from all over the world who felt the same way I did. It's always nice to get feedback from people online, but it was so much more than that.

Quilt Pattern 1

I was so shy at the time, but I decided to start a modern quilt group where I invited strangers into my home to talk about quilts. This may sound very odd, but I trusted that quilters were good people, and they are! They are fabulous, generous, and sharing people. For the first two years of running the guild, I would sweat and shake when I had to act as a leader. I never thought I would be comfortable speaking in public, but the guild gave me a chance to express myself. It changed me from a shy person who didn't like being looked at into a confident, creative woman with a voice.

I was so grateful from the experience that I decided to give back the joy and the confidence I was gaining through quilting. I started asking other quilters, through my blog, to help me in providing quilts for homeless families and for other situations as they arose. Now, not only do I get up and speak about all you fabulous people who donate, but I get to meet complete strangers by handing them a quilt and giving them a hug. This experience of giving back to the community is up high on my must-do list. The process of making a quilt gives me great satisfaction, but giving away a quilt? There is nothing better.

Favorite Quote

"We cannot think of being acceptable to others until we have first proven acceptable to ourselves."

– Malcom X

Quilting has brought my community of people to me. I no longer wonder who I am and where am I going. Quilting makes me very happy; it has led me to a good place spiritually, emotionally, and creatively. It has connected me with people who I might have never met, and I've discovered what I truly need to be happy. If I can give one needy person a quilt or a fellow quilter a spark of confidence in themselves to do the same, then I know have done something right in my life.

To learn more about Victoria Findlay Wolfe, visit bumblebeansinc. com, 15minutesplay.com, *and* bumblebeansbasics.com.

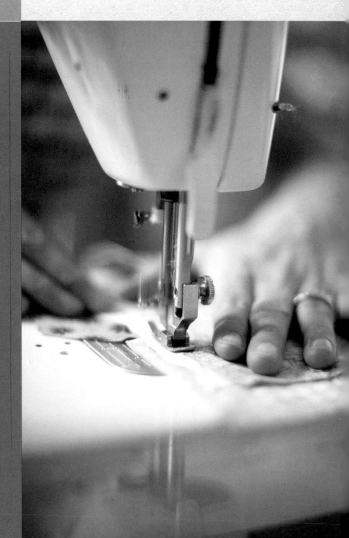

173

Credits

Images on pages 174 and 175 are Brigitte Heitland by Hilla Südhaus.

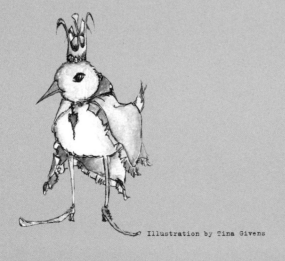

Illustration by Tina Givens